Archery : the modern approach

ARCHERY
the modern approach

E. G. HEATH

Faber and Faber Limited
London · Boston

First published in 1978
by Faber and Faber Limited
3 Queen Square London WC1
Printed in Great Britain by
Latimer Trend & Company Ltd Plymouth

British Library Cataloguing in Publication Data

Heath, Ernest Gerald
Archery.—New ed
1. Archery
I. Title
799.3'2 GV1185

ISBN 0-571-04957-5
ISBN 0-571-11168-8 Pbk

Contents

	Introduction	*page* 11
1	Equipped to Shoot	13
2	The Appeal of Archery	32
3	Variety in Archery	39
4	Learning to Shoot—1	54
5	Learning to Shoot—2	86
6	Etiquette and Safety	101
7	The Club	109
8	The Tournament	124
9	Archery International	143
	Appendix A Target Rounds	153
	Appendix B Useful Addresses	155

List of Illustrations

1a	Longbow cross-section	*page* 14
1b	Cross-section of Asiatic composite bow	16
1c	Cross-section of modern composite bow	17
2	Parts of a bow	20
3	The Archer's Paradox	21
4	Parts of an arrow	23
5	Checking arrow length	24
6	Arrow fletchings	26
7	Archer's Knot	27
8	The bracer	29
9	The shooting tab	29
10	Wheelchair archer	34
11	5-zone target face	40
12	10-zone target faces	41
13	Field Round target faces	46
14	Flight shooting	49
15	Bracing a practice bow	60
16	Bracing a composite bow	61
17	Using a bow stringer	62
18	String loop and bow nock	62
19	Standing	66
20	Nocking—first method	67
21	Nocking—second method	68
22	Fingers on string	69
23	The Preparation Position	70
24	Drawing—method one	73
25	Drawing—method two	74

26	Drawing—method three	75
27	The anchor point	76
28	Full draw	78
29	Follow through	84
30	Checking the dominant eye	86
31	The principles of aiming	89
32	Aiming—one	90
33	Aiming—two	90
34	Arrows high	96
35	Arrows low	96
36	Arrows right	97
37	Arrows left	97
38	Drawing arrows from a target	107
39	G.N.A.S. badge	110
40	Score sheet	123
41	Measuring a best gold	128
42	Archery field layout	137
43	F.I.T.A. badge	144

Introduction to Second Edition

'It is absolutely necessary that the archer should take up his bow with coolness and attention, for haste and too great eagerness are qualities in an archer which must be got rid of, before he can arrive at any degree of excellence in the art.'

T. ROBERTS, 1801

As a pastime with appeal to every taste and ambition archery has no parallel and once the basic principles of shooting have been mastered the archer will soon realize that the skills learned so far can be applied in different ways. A great amount of pleasure can be experienced by archers who shoot purely for the joy of it, finding relaxation in the leisured rhythm of bending a bow in the amiable company of others so inclined. Alternatively a large proportion of archers strive for progressively higher standards by serious study and practical application. To be proficient at making consistently good scores is far more satisfying than to struggle like a dunce whose performance never improves, but as with all sporting pursuits proficiency depends, to a large extent, on practice and study. The amount of practice and the degree of study will depend on the facilities available, the time at the disposal of the archer and individual ambition.

Since this book appeared in its original form the sport of archery has seen many changes, and this second edition has been substantially revised to take into account improvements in techniques, equipment, rules, and up-to-date methods of pursuing the art of shooting in a bow. Much of the historical background, which appeared earlier, has been deleted—not for the reason that this information is superfluous, far from it, because archers have always treasured the traditions of their sport, but for the reason that these matters have been more thoroughly dealt with in subsequent books by this author than space would allow in the present work.

The skills of archery have become more exacting, and the sport itself has been taken up by archers from all parts of the world in greater numbers than ever before. This in itself is an achievement in internationalism, due in most part to the drive and enthusiasm of the World Archery Federation, a body still relatively young. The international character of archery has been specially dealt with in a new chapter.

Opportunities for wider competition have been encouraged and this, together with technological improvements in equipment, has resulted in rapidly rising scores. However, the archer's skill does not improve solely through the spirit of competition and the use of better weapons—themselves important factors—higher standards depend essentially on better and more systemized coaching methods. For those taking up the sport for the first time there is no short cut to superlative shooting, it is a question of learning the rudiments, developing an individual approach, understanding the multiplicity of matters necessary for good shooting, and practice, practice, practice. Many of these matters are dealt with in detail in this book, and guidance is given to those who intend pursuing archery in any of its aspects. The same principles of technique and methods of shooting apply, whether the intention is to seek the exacting standards of international competition or whether the sport is to be treated as a relaxing pastime. Whatever the aim, those who take up archery embark on a unique experience, and the over-all intention of this book is to give encouragement to those who do so.

1 · Equipped to Shoot

Anyone eager to take up archery would be well advised to familiarize himself with the various items of equipment used, the specialized terminology of archery, and the simple mechanics of shooting arrows from a bow before actually attempting to shoot. By assimilating some general background knowledge the beginner may avoid finding the actual moment of facing a target for the first time so strange as it might have been otherwise.

Many of the technical aspects can be read, mused over, and forgotten, but the nomenclature of archery in general use is worth extra study; archers' discussions, even of the least profound nature, would be unusual if they were not liberally sprinkled with references to matters peculiar to archery and terminology which sounds completely foreign to the uninitiated.

The unparalleled increase in the use of bows and arrows as a sporting pastime during the past forty years and the technological advance made during that period are probably unique in sports history. Detailed accounts of these developments are available, but an outline of the main aspects should be sufficient for all but the engineer or scientist.

The technical background

Though unchanged in principle the instruments of archery today differ profoundly in detail from their ancient prototypes. Changes in design, materials and construction have produced bows and arrows radically different from those used during the first decades of this century, and in the hands of skilful users modern equipment gives a performance never before known.

The transformation of design from the old to the new began in the 1930s, principally through research and experiment by two Americans, C. N. Hickman and Professor P. E. Klopsteg. Their scientific investigations undoubtedly formed the foundation of modern bow design which rapidly found favour with archers of the western world. Such matters which were investigated included the effects of the shape, dimensions, relative settings and angles of bow limbs on the performance of the bow, factors which determine arrow movement, velocity and trajectory, the geometry and methods of aiming and even the psychological factors in shooting.

The two representative types of bow from which the kind now generally used has evolved are the longbow, with which are associated centuries of history and tradition, and the Asiatic composite bow. The longbow had straight limbs when relaxed, i.e. not strung. The limbs terminated in fitted tips of horn with grooves (nocks) in which the loops of the string were seated. Limbs tapered in both width and thickness from grip to tip. At any cross-section the limb was rounded on the belly side, towards the string, and more or less flattened on the back, the opposite side. In the drawn bow the belly is under compression, the back under tension. A typical cross-section of a limb of a longbow is shown in Fig. 1 (a). Such a limb is said to be 'stacked' and was

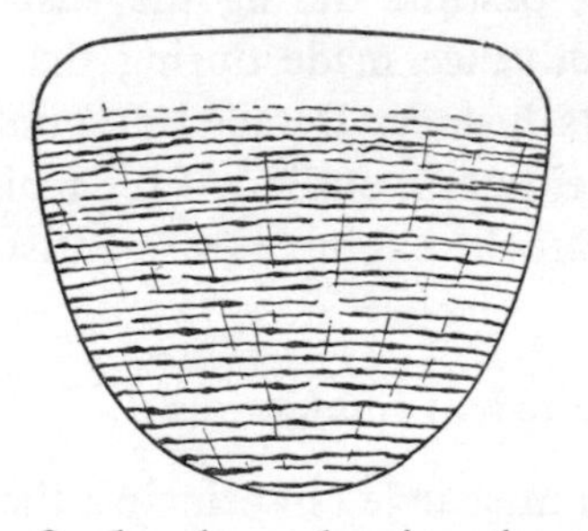

Section of
traditional
English longbow

Fig. 1a Typical cross-section of a longbow showing the sapwood (light) forming the back of the bow, the remainder being heartwood

a violation of good mechanical principles in not properly exploiting the possibilities of the wood from which the bow was fashioned. A bow of this type had to be long to minimize stresses and prevent breakage; hence 'longbow'. The grip occupied the region where the tapering limbs merged, and bending occurred throughout the length of the bow; for this reason an unpleasant recoil might be felt in the bow hand when the arrow was loosed. Up to the 1930s the only change in design seems to have been one intended to reduce this recoil. This change consisted of making the grip rigid and unbending by leaving more wood in the handle portion.

Modern equipment

In realizing the theoretical shortcomings of the longbow the early experimenters were convinced that better bows could be made, and very soon the flat bow was designed which proved about twice as efficient as the longbow. This was a bow rectangular in section which, briefly, had the effect of loading the limbs uniformly, and made possible a reduction of length by 10 to 15 per cent while reducing the hazard of breakage. This new development met with some scepticism from tradition-bound archers, but it also met with widely increasing acceptance. It is today the basic design for inexpensive bows made of wood or of fibre-glass used extensively for practice purposes.

A development which had a very popular and widespread acceptance was the introduction of a bow of tubular steel construction. The pioneers of this revolutionary advance were a Swedish firm with a specialized sports division, and the steel bow, which had the added advantage of coming apart for easy carriage, made its first appearance on the shooting line as somewhat of a novelty, but when scores were compared it was soon apparent that this product of precision engineering was responsible for greater accuracy and therefore better performances from individuals. The demand for this new bow grew rapidly and British manufacturers soon established departments to design, produce and market these bows. The decline of the steel bow, which had in its turn completely ousted the longbow, was marked by the introduction to British archers of the modern composite bow in the mid-1950s. Some slight progress and experimentation had been made in this country with backings of man-made materials but the major contribution to the design and development of the modern composite bow came from America.

The Asiatic composite bow differed profoundly from its English contemporary counterpart. Whereas the longbow was made exclusively of wood, the oriental composite had limbs construc-

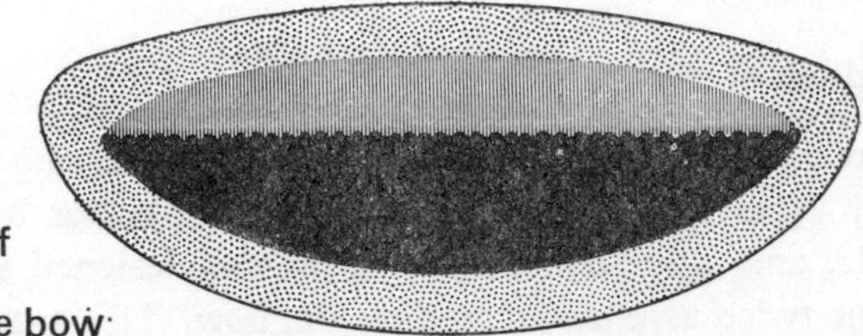

Fig. 1b Cross-section of an Asiatic composite bow which shows a central core of wood (shaded) and horn (dark) covered with layers of shredded sinew

ted of materials in layers, so arranged that the compression, tension and shear in the bent limbs occurred in those materials best adapted to withstand these respective forces. Horn, which is compressible, was used as the belly of the bow, sinew, which has elastic properties, was used for the back, and the whole was built up on a wooden core and covered with moisture-proof lacquers. The ultimate in composite bows were beautifully constructed and had quite extraordinary performance records [see Fig. 1 (b)]. Many American archers interested in flight shooting became interested in Asiatic bowyery and improved their bows by adding sinew backs, a process not unknown to some American Indian tribes, and fitting stiff 'ears' to the ends of their shortened bows. These improvements increased flight distances out of the 400s of yards and into the 500s.

Research and development during and after the war produced plastics with excellent characteristics for reliably storing and releasing energy through stress loading and unloading. Mass production at low cost of glass fibres was perfected, making long parallel fibres of glass readily available. Applications of these new materials were soon perfected and horn and sinew have been displaced by strong plastics with fibre-glass reinforcements.

The modern bow has limbs rectangular in section, with adequate width to ensure stability against twisting as the bow is drawn. The design is aimed at employing the whole limb, including the backwardly curved ends, for storing energy, and each

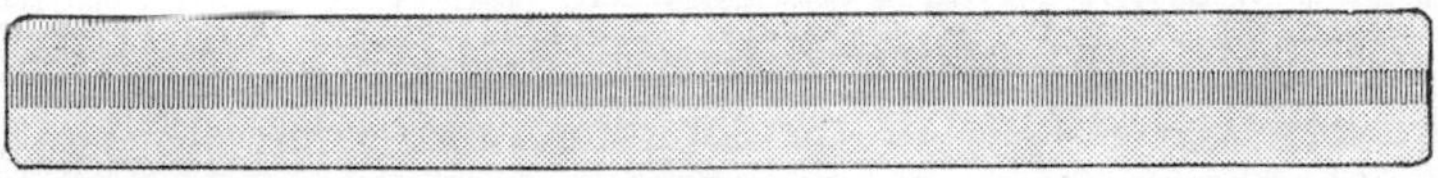

Section of
modern
composite bow

Fig. 1c Cross-section of modern composite bow with a central core of wood with laminations of fibre-glass on the back and the belly of the bow

limb 'works' throughout with approximately the same stored energy in each unit of volume of the stressed limb. The limbs are built up on a thin strip of wood, usually hard maple, to both sides of which the plastic with embedded glass fibres is bonded [see Fig. 1 (c)]. The new construction has relative immunity to normal temperature and humidity variations and there is little or no tendency to follow the string, i.e., to take a permanent set from being braced and drawn. It may be braced over long periods, and when relaxed will resume its original form. A feature which has many variations is the sculptured grip, first developed to accommodate an archer with a weakened wrist, and now shaped to ensure that the force applied by the bow hand has a constant location.

The latest developments in bow design incorporate various devices for stabilizing 'torque'—the turning force which occurs in the bow when shot, and these generally take the form of weighted rods projecting from the back of the bow, away from the archer. Adjustable sights are available in a wide variety of design and many of the more advanced patterns are precision instruments in themselves. Several manufacturers have introduced take-apart composite bows in recent years, which generally consist of a centre handle section of lightweight magnesium to which bow limbs are locked and bolted. The advantages which are claimed for this type of bow include the ease with which the limbs can be interchanged or replaced according to the archer's needs, and the strength and lightness provided by the use of alloy compared with wood.

The bow of the 1970s is composite in Asiatic tradition, though in modified form, influenced by the designs which developed from research studies of the longbow, and improved by the practical application of scientific investigations into ballistics and engineering principles.

The modern arrow also makes its contribution to accuracy. Wooden arrows which have been largely superseded were extremely difficult to match for weight, spine and characteristics, and this was approximated by a lengthy selection process. Arrows are now made of strong aluminium alloy tubing, precision drawn, with constant physical properties such as stiffness and mass per unit length for each diameter and wall thickness. Yet another variable factor, that of drag, has been eliminated in replacing natural feathers with vanes of plastic.

The new bows and arrows have added immeasurably to the potential enjoyment of the sport and have opened up the pleasures of archery to many who would have found the traditional equipment too exasperating to manage. However, the old-fashioned equipment still holds a special exhilaration for some, often archers of many years standing, who are unwilling or unable to give time for the long and arduous practice needed to attain high scores, and who would, even with the finest equipment money can buy, scarcely improve their standard. For such archers there is the added fascination of having to learn the characteristic behaviour of each bow and each arrow in even slight variations of climate and wind. They each seem to have their own personality which must be humoured.

The bow

The various parts of the bow are shown in Fig. 2. Dependent on its construction the bow may have limbs which vary slightly in length. In a bow of simple construction the hand-grip is placed off-centre so that the arrow is shot from a position only slightly above the centre of the bow; this means, therefore, that the lower limb is shorter than the upper. When the string is drawn the fingers are placed above and below the arrow which results in extra pull being exerted on the lower nock, as a compromise the bottom limb is made a little stiffer so that both limbs come to the same curve at full draw. Bows of more complex design have the space used by the bow handle offset by a solid and much longer centre construction which allows for the limbs to be short and fast to react, and to be identical in length and springiness. Composite bows have the limb tips reinforced and carefully grooved plus an additional few inches of channel in which the string lies when the bow is braced.

The shape of the grip or bow-handle has developed from the simple form of thickening of a riser (a double-wedge-shaped piece of hardwood around which a wrapping of leather or similar non-slip material is added for comfort), to sculptured grips which have become standard features in today's composite bows. The contours of these modern bow handles are extremely varied in shape and are devised as a result of field trials by archer-bowyers and, one is tempted to suggest, by the caprice of the manufacturer. A popular pattern is the so-called 'pistol' grip, but the variations in this style alone defy complete enumeration. The essential feature in all these shapes is that so long as the archer can find a comfortable grip which suits his particular style it matters little whether the craftsman has merely added a slight bulge or has produced a bow-handle reminiscent of some of the more extravagant modern abstract sculptures. Features which are now incorporated in the shaping of the bow which add considerably to the technical efficiency of the weapon and to the personal comfort of the archer include an arrow-rest and semi centre-shot designs. In using modern self bows for practice pur-

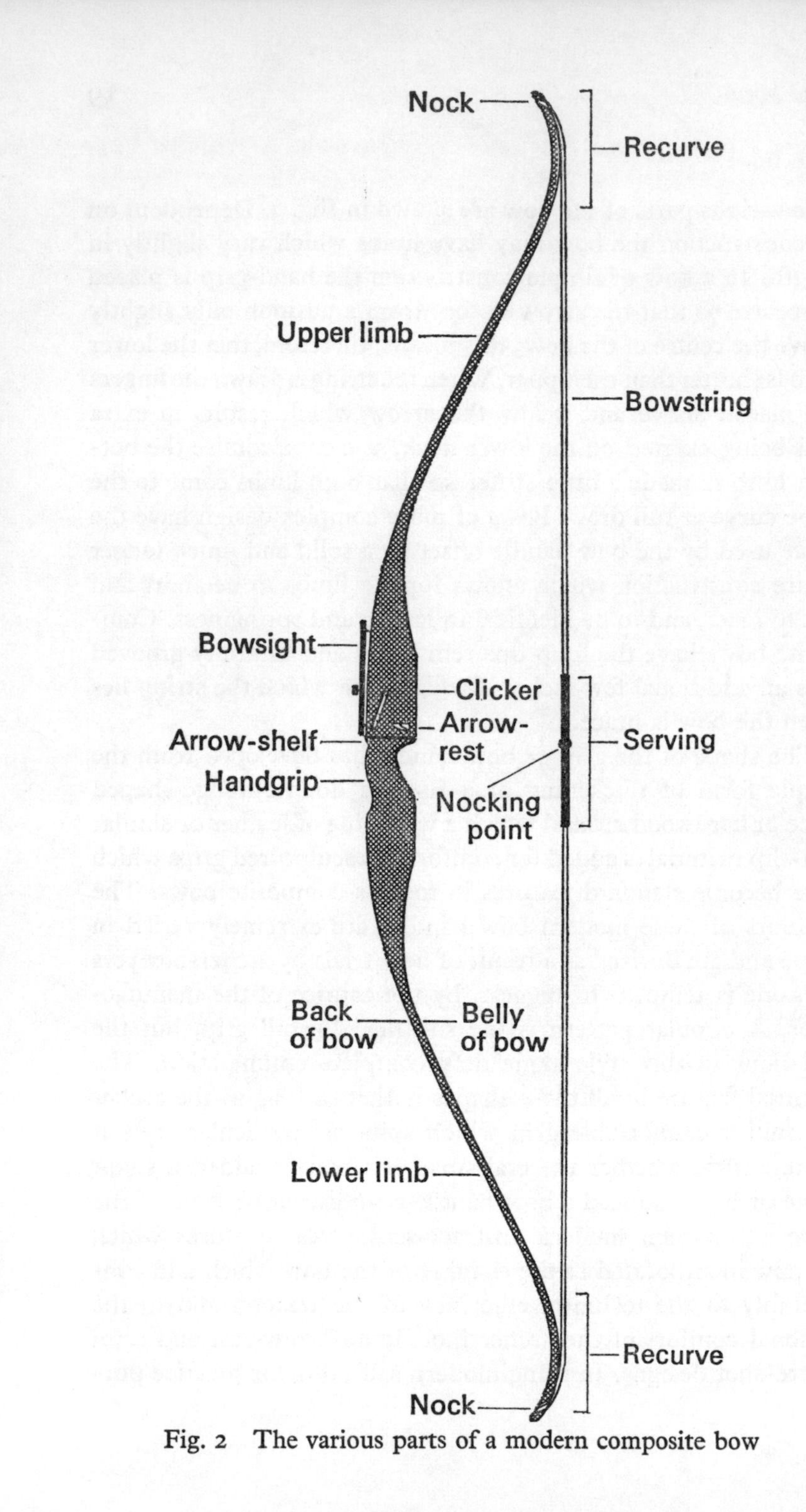

Fig. 2 The various parts of a modern composite bow

poses, and longbows, the arrow is rested on, and drawn back across, the ledge formed when the hand grasps the bow. This can have serious disadvantages if a slight difference in grip position is adopted, for to be accurately shot arrows need to be exactly positioned each time the bow is drawn. The advantage of a fixed arrow-rest is plain to see. By constructing a bow so that an arrow shot from it leaves from the centre of the width of the limb, a phenomenon known as the Archer's Paradox, is almost completely eliminated.

The archer's paradox

In operating a simple bow, although the released string returns to rest in a direct line with the central axis of the bow limbs, the arrow changes its line of direction in a manner quite considerable due to the thickness of the bow limb deflecting it from a direct line. This is somewhat perplexing for the archer who has not had

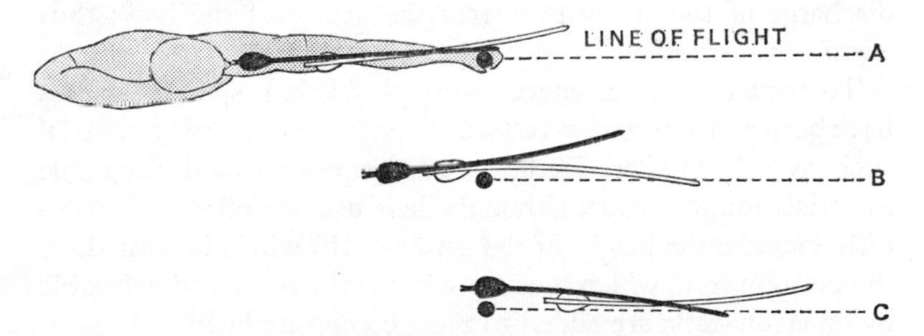

Fig. 3 The Archer's Paradox, a bird's eye view

this mysterious matter explained to him. In Fig. 3 (a) the arrow is shown fully drawn and it will be seen that, on release, although the string returns to rest in line with the bow carrying the arrow before it, due to the width of the bow limb the shaft will deflect from the line of flight quite considerably before the string has completed its journey. The initial impact of the released string on the arrow actually bends it towards and then away from the side of the bow (Fig. 3 (b)) and this bending continues during the time the string is pushing forward. The arrow curves round the bow, its fletchings nicely clearing all obstacles (Fig. 3 (c)). Once clear of the bow and free of the string the arrow rights itself by springing back to bend in the reverse plane and continues a series of diminishing oscillations until it is flying on its original and intended course.

This problem has been studied rather more than other archery phenomena and several slow-motion cine films, taken under laboratory conditions, have added to our knowledge of arrow flight and contributed greatly to improved bow design. A reduction in the amount of deflection can be effected by adjusting the width of the bow at the point where the arrow leaves it, the advantage being that the amount of oscillation required to clear the bow is reduced to the minimum and the problems of the Archer's Paradox begin to fade, and consequently matching of arrows to bow is simplified. Modern bow design incorporates cut-away portions of the centre section which have reduced the width of the bow having the effect of adjusting the position of the discharge of the arrow to nearer the centre of the bow: thus 'semi centre-shot'.

To reduce losses in energy through friction, special surfaces have been added to arrow-rests, and the fashion for using material such as soft bristles, feathers—edge upwards, and deep pile materials found favour, although their use can often imperceptibly increase the height of the arrow-shelf, which in turn alters the position from which the arrow leaves the bow. Today flexible nylon arrow-rests are added to most composite bows.

Selection of equipment

Bows are measured according to the weight needed to extend them to full draw in pounds avoirdupois. Thus if a bow is made for use with 28-inch arrows its weight is measured at this draw length and if arrows of a lesser length are used the effective poundage is proportionately reduced. The size of arrows for which the bow is made is always specified in addition to its weight, and, although shorter arrows can be used, on no account can arrows be used which are longer than those specified for the bow.

The Arrow

The names given to the particular parts of the arrow are shown in Fig. 4. Modern refinements have produced a target missile improvements to which are hard to imagine. The essential points to be borne in mind when a beginner chooses his first set of

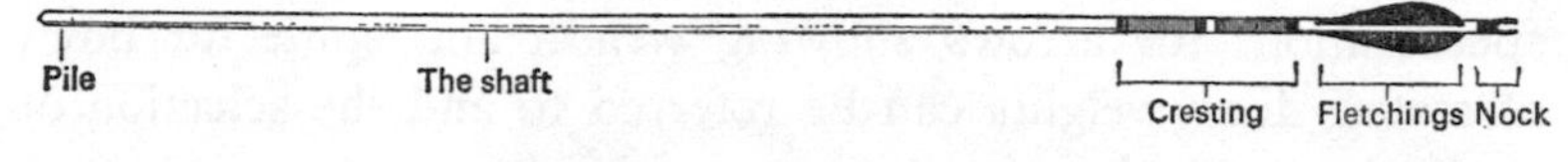

Fig. 4 The parts of a tournament arrow

arrows are three: that they match the bow which he is to use; that they match him; and that they are the best he can afford. The majority of target arrows used today are made of a high-quality alloy tube of high tensile strength, and although they can suffer damage by bending they can be straightened quite successfully by the archer himself or by the manufacturer. Fibre-glass tubes have found some popularity and they have proved most efficient as arrowshafts, their greatest advantage being that they do not take a permanent set when bent. However, they are relatively expensive. Both the above materials have almost completely ousted the only type of arrow known for centuries, made of wood which, however, is still widely used by field archers.

The successful discharge of an arrow depends entirely on its being correctly matched to the bow, and this is effected by the accurate combination of three factors, 'spine', weight and length. 'Spine' can be defined as the measurement of an arrow's resistance to bending, or its degree of suppleness—this is measured in hundredths of an inch when a weight is suspended from the centre of an arrow which is supported at nock and pile. The standards for measuring spine vary but in this country the weight used is $1\frac{1}{2}$ lb. When purchasing arrows the choice of correct spine is of paramount importance, if the arrow is too stiff it will fly badly and probably will not clear the bow on release, if too supple or 'limber' it will be erratic in direction and have a character difficult to control.

The weight of arrows is related progressively to the draw weight of bows and is measured in grains. The old-fashioned scale of measurement was by weight of silver coins. A 'five-shilling' arrow for instance was one that balanced a scale on the opposite pan of which were five shilling pieces, and often one can still read the weight marked in this fashion on arrows used with longbows. Modern arrows in a matched set have a tolerance of weight of as little as one grain between them. Detailed tables of specifications for arrows showing weight and spine for bows of stated draw-weights can be referred to and the selection of correctly matched arrows becomes a simple matter.

Formerly two arrow lengths were generally available, 28 inches for gentlemen and 25 inches for ladies, which must have been delightfully uncomplicated for the archery stockist but most

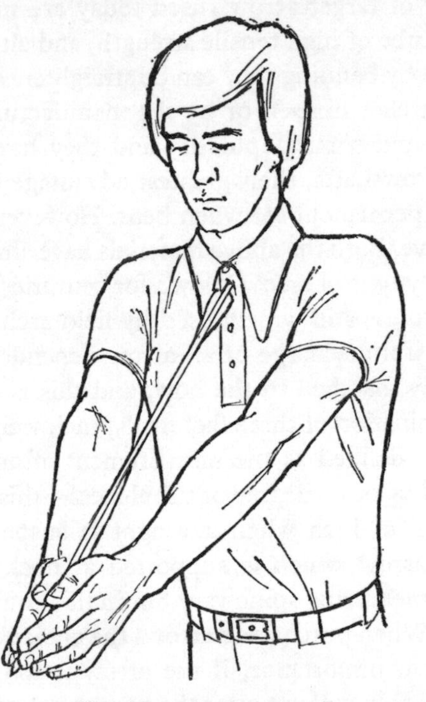

Fig. 5 Checking the length of an arrow

restricting for the individual archer; today, however, arrows in lengths from 21 inches increasing by half inches to 30 inches are readily available. To determine the length of arrow required a measurement should be taken from the throat to the tips of the outstretched fingers when the arms are extended together straight out in front of the archer. This measurement may increase slightly as the various muscles become more accustomed to the activity of drawing a bow, and this should be taken into consideration when selecting arrows. For target use arrows are normally supplied in sets of eight, although only six are used, two being kept as spares. A satisfactory rule of thumb method of assessing a suitable arrow length is demonstrated in Fig. 5.

Fletchings are the means whereby the arrows are steadied in flight and, if feathers are used, perform a secondary function in that they impart to the arrow a slight spin as it is in motion. On examination it will be seen that a feather has a unique natural feature, one side has a smooth, shiny appearance and the other a slightly coarser, ribbed look. Nature constructed them in this fashion as part of the wonderful flying apparatus of birds, helping to provide what is known aeronautically as lift. These surfaces arranged lengthwise produce a lift which is transferred into a rotary motion in an arrow. Right and left wing feathers are constructed in opposite patterns, thus in fletching an arrow feathers from one wing only must be used, otherwise opposing air currents will be set up which will ruin the flight of an arrow. To accentuate the spinning motion in an arrow feathers are often set on spirally. This is a practice which is frequently employed by field archers and hunters to reduce the possibility of 'planing' when a broadhead is used and to minimize deflection if a cross-wind is blowing. A certain amount of spiral in the setting of fletchings is said by some to have an advantageous effect in target shooting, but the degree of improvement, if any, would be so slight that it would hardly be noticed by the average archer. Although the universally accepted number of vanes is three (see Fig. 6), 4-fletch and other multiple fletching arrangements have been experimented with; again the improvements in performance are only perceptible to a very experienced archer shooting to high standards. Widely

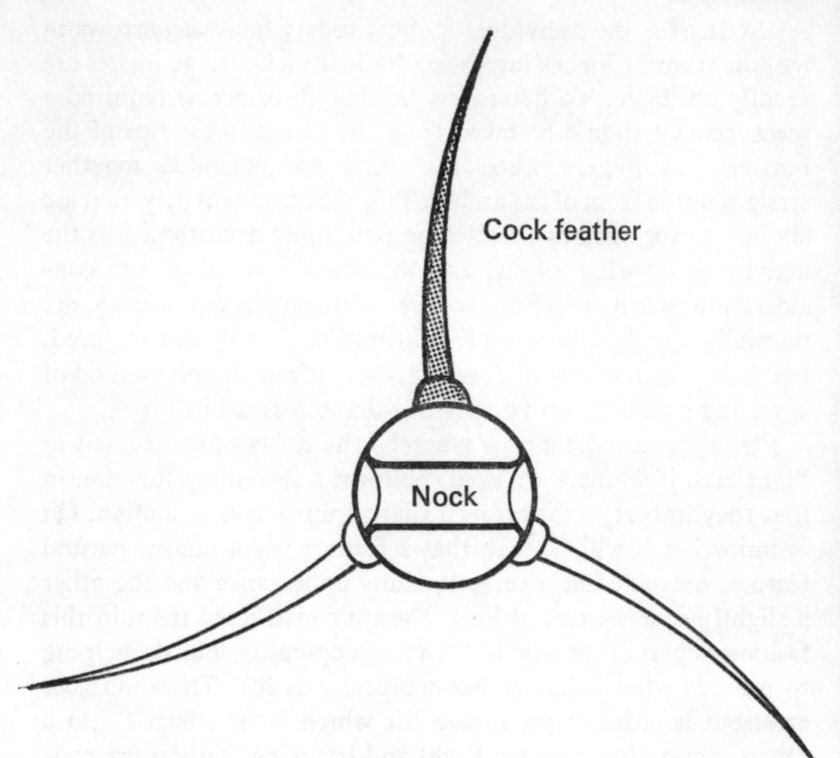

Fig. 6 The arrangement of fletchings on an arrow. Note that the cock feather, often a contrasting colour, is set at right-angles to the slot of the nock

ranging colour combinations of fletchings can be obtained and archers can select their own particular pattern of cresting colours to match. The cresting in front of the fletching, which sometimes used to be the personal heraldic colours of the owner, is used, together with the name or initials of the archer painted on the shaftment of the arrow, to assist identification when several archers are shooting together on the same target.

The performance of a bow varies according to the user's technique and physical attributes. Techniques can be acquired through careful study and enjoyable practice, but an individual's physique cannot be changed. The satisfactory operation of archery equipment can only be assured if it is of specifications in proportion to the archer's stature and physique. Care must be taken to ensure that the choice of equipment is quite suitable for the person who intends using it. For the beginner a bow of light draw-weight is advisable, from 26 to 32 lb. for men and 22 to 30 lb. for ladies should be quite sufficient. Such a bow will not reach the longer tournament distances but it will reward its user by being capable of easy management and by not being responsible for early frustration and fatigue that would be produced by a bow which is too strong for its owner. It is far better to purchase one of the moderately priced self bows, which are sometimes termed practice bows, for the introductory period of archery. An alternative to a self wood bow is the solid fibre-glass bow, which has gained popularity in recent years as a beginner's bow. It is moderately priced and virtually indestructible. When the archer becomes more proficient and decides to progress to more elaborate and more expensive equipment, a careful study of the types available with, if possible, trials of several will be an advantage.

Bowstrings

The string of a bow is made to exact measurements to fit the bow for which it is intended. For practice wooden bows and longbows strings are made of linen, a number of strands of which, of a known breaking strain, are formed into a rope; a tail is made at one end and a permanent loop is spliced at the other. The tail is used to form the lower loop by tying what is popularly called the Archer's Knot, actually a Timber Hitch (see Fig. 7). This is easily adjusted so that the string can be lengthened or shortened

Fig. 7 The Archer's Knot (a standard Timber Hitch)

as required. Sometimes a second loop is made instead of a tail. A central section of the string is protected by a serving of thicker thread and the precise point of nocking is slightly thickened by a wrapping of waxed silk thread, or what is more often used today, dental floss, which can be obtained in conveniently small quantities. This additional binding is known as the nocking point. Reinforcements of thread are added to the loops and the whole is given an application of beeswax which serves to preserve the string's natural moisture, on which flax relies for strength, and helps the threads to adhere to each other.

Man-made fibres are used today to make double-loop endless bowstrings which are used on solid fibre-glass and composite bows. The making of these strings consists of utilizing one length of thread of Fortisan or Dacron and forming a number of turns of the exact measurement required; the loops are included as an integral part of this construction. There is extra reinforcement on the loops and this, together with the centre serving and nocking point is finished in a similar fashion to the linen string of the single loop type.

In use a bowstring must be occasionally inspected, and if any signs of deterioration appear, such as fraying, it should immediately be discarded and a fresh one fitted. To have two strings to one's bow should be interpreted by archers quite literally—one in use and one spare.

Bracers, tabs and quivers

In addition to the bow and arrows certain essential items of personal equipment are required for every archer and the most important are the bracer and the shooting tab or glove. Until the proper method of holding a bow is learnt and the correct arm position found the released bowstring can often strike the inside of the novice's forearm with painful results or it may foul loose clothing. The bracer is worn on the bow-arm as a protection against such minor disasters. A piece of smooth but tough leather fastened with a couple of straps is all that is required, but any suitable material can be used provided that no sharp edges present themselves against which the string may be frayed. Excellent bracers of varying designs and alternative materials are commercially available although some archers prefer to make their own (see Fig. 8).

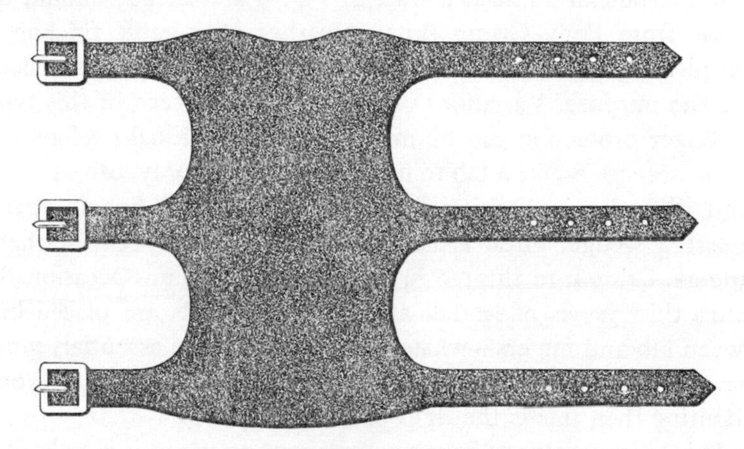

Fig. 8 A popular form of leather bracer

The shooting tab is the form of finger-tip protection worn by the majority of archers today; the remainder use gloves with reinforced finger-tips. The use of a shooting tab, 'made to measure', of tough but supple leather and with a good smooth surface is the first requisite for a clean loose. Great care must be taken to ensure that the tab or glove fits perfectly, as by this an archer can succeed or fail. A badly fitting tab or the use of one

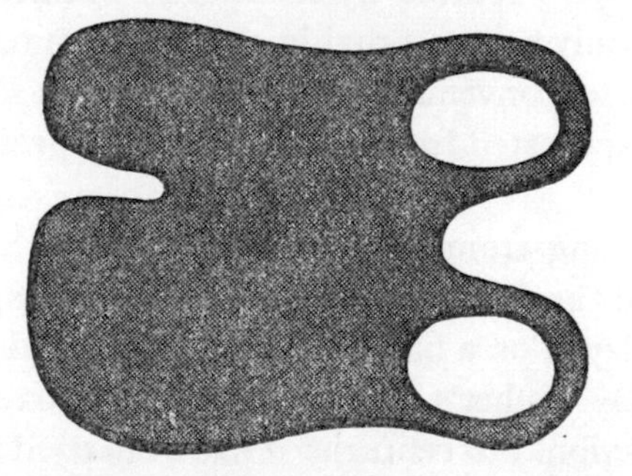

Fig. 9 A simple shooting tab for a three-fingered loose

which has been hastily borrowed can have a disastrous effect on the loose and any discomfort caused by the prolonged use of a tight or ill-fitting glove is, to say the least, very disconcerting. The most general design of tab used for the 3-fingered or 'Mediterranean' loose is shown in Fig. 9 and ideally should be made from Pony Crupp Butt, a leather of suitable thickness, suppleness, and toughness, which has been found to be excellent for the purpose. Variations of the standard pattern of this type of finger protection can be made to suit individual preference; some archers prefer a tab to fit over one finger only, others, who find difficulty in keeping their first and second fingers apart, insert a wedge, often a small loop of leather, between these fingers, fixing it to the tab in the correct position. Occasionally extra thicknesses of leather and other materials are placed between tab and fingers—whatever the pattern the essentials must be met and providing the result proves to be efficient for your shooting then this is the right pattern for you.

It is as important to have a spare shooting tab as it is to have a spare bowstring. A borrowed tab never fits properly and it is well-nigh impossible for a barefingered archer to shoot a complete round without considerable discomfort.

Today most archers use a quiver. For target archery several types are in general use normally slung from the belt, but for field shooting a quiver specially designed to sling on the archer's back is more popular. Very often the results of industrious winter evenings are exhibited in the individually designed and beautifully made quivers sported by handicraft-minded archers. The function of a quiver is to provide a temporary resting place for the arrows in use, convenient of access and often so designed that each arrow is separated from its neighbour to prevent damage to fletchings.

One item slung from the archer's belt which often attracts comment from the uninitiated is the tassel. As a splash of colour perfectly displayed on a background of green and white clothing the present-day archer's tassel has a decorative as well as a utilitarian function. For centuries it has been used to clean arrows of any dirt which would otherwise affect their flight, and nowadays tassels are made up in club colours, a central register of which is maintained for clubs in this country.

Archers are particularly apt to devise and use gadgets both ingenious and frivolous, and any shooting line can provide a crop of such extra items which do not appear in any text book or equipment catalogue. They are not essentials, but so long as they provide the means of better enjoyment of the sport and do not contravene the Rules of Shooting in force at the time there can be no objection to them.

It is almost instinctive for an archer to be practical and this quality is an undoubted asset. Apart from the actual making of bows and arrows the general maintenance and handling of these simple but fascinating weapons is no job for the careless or ham-fisted. First know your tackle—then care for it: such devotion will be repaid with faithful service and many pleasurable hours of healthful recreation combined with a special, quite personal, exhilaration when a man, bow, and arrow work as one.

Apart from the regulations for the Grand National Archery Meeting, the National Target Championships, and the International Trial, no specific form of dress is laid down for archery in the United Kingdom. However, guidance is given as to the accepted dress which should be encouraged whenever organized shooting takes place, which, 'For ladies is skirt, blouse, and when required, a sweater or cardigan, and for gentlemen is trousers, shirt and/or a sweater, in plain dark green and white. There is no objection to wearing green garments and white garments together.' Waterproof clothing, worn only during wet weather, is not subject to regulations, but both green and white waterproofs are recommended. Green is a colour traditionally associated with archery and specifications for the recommended greens are British Colour Council Bottle Green No. 25, Tartan Green No. 26, and Rifle Green No. 27. There is something particularly English about a line of archers dressed in green and white shooting at colourful targets against a background of ancient trees in full leaf, a heritage worthy of preservation.

2 · The Appeal of Archery

The foregoing chapter will have given the tyro a general impression of the apparatus of archery; let him (or her) now discover some of the more important and sometimes little known features of the sport which give to it a unique and universal appeal. To publicize archery certain aspects of it are generally used, one being emphasis on the fact that it attracts members of both sexes and all ages and is quite often most suitable for disabled persons as an aid to rehabilitation. As far as age is concerned it will be obvious that, generally speaking, the best shots will be in their prime of life and of course in this respect bodily fitness plays its part. But a very large contingent of the 'old brigade' of archers still find extreme pleasure in shooting in a bow. The pleasures of the archery field are hard to resist and even more difficult to give up, and although it is not commonplace one occasionally hears of archers in their eighties still shooting, and in recent years archers even in their nineties have been known and admired for their tenacious skills. At the other end of the scale youngsters to whom the fascination of archery seems to be a perennial attraction have a natural aptitude for handling a bow and arrow and much has been done to encourage them to follow in the footsteps of their legendary heroes, although with a little more restraint. A rational explanation of the legendary exploits of Robin Hood for instance, which, despite their incredibility, are inextricably linked with historical fact, will teach a child to respect the bow as a weapon and not as a toy.

Archery for schools

Scholastic institutions have long recognized the importance of organized games and sports, and archery is included in the curriculum of many schools. The Association for Archery in Schools, formed in 1963, is a body which attends to the needs of youthful archers by the general promotion of the sport, arranging tournaments and so on, activities which otherwise would have possibly been neglected by organizations mainly devoted to adult archery. The A.A.S. runs a summer postal league, which is open to teams of four juniors, and an inter-schools Team Tournament held annually at the end of the season. Both these events are well supported which indicates the enthusiasm and interest amongst budding World Champions. In addition this association has recently introduced the Archery Achievement Scheme, open to juniors not only within this organization, but also to those who are members of properly affiliated archery clubs generally. Juniors who reach certain standards can qualify for badge awards, which indicate their progress in the sport. The Duke of Edinburgh's Award Scheme for boys and girls includes archery as a 'pursuit' for boys and an 'interest' for girls, and for a candidate to qualify he or she has to satisfy examiners as to his or her aptitude and enthusiasm in accordance with an official syllabus which is far from arduous or difficult. A candidate needs to be an enthusiastic archer and a trier but not necessarily a good shot. Through this scheme, which is designed to prepare boys and girls for good citizenship, many youngsters not only learn the art of archery but, in addition, learn how to become useful club members.

Junior championships for archers under eighteen years of age are held annually for which a series of officially recognized rounds were devised in 1963. Known as the 'Bristol' School of Rounds they have been based on the York and Hereford Rounds which are used for adult championships and are arranged so that allowances are made between boys and girls and age groups of juniors.

In addition to the special arrangements necessary for the inclusion of young people in the normal pattern of modern archery the Grand National Archery Society is the first to recognize the importance of encouraging juniors to take up the bow, for with the passing of but a few years boys and girls become men and women and in many cases their archery activities continue into their adult lives, or perhaps, even though temporarily set aside for other new-found grown-up pleasures, are taken up again a year or so later.

Disabled archers

Medical authorities have accepted archery as a most valuable aid to rehabilitation for particular classes of disability. It is taught in hospitals as a remedial exercise particularly for those disabled as a result of a spinal disorder and who are confined to wheelchairs. Archery is one of the very few sports in which the disabled can compete on equal terms with the able-bodied, and the G.N.A.S., recognizing this fact, allows archers so handicapped every facility to enable them to shoot in any type of match or

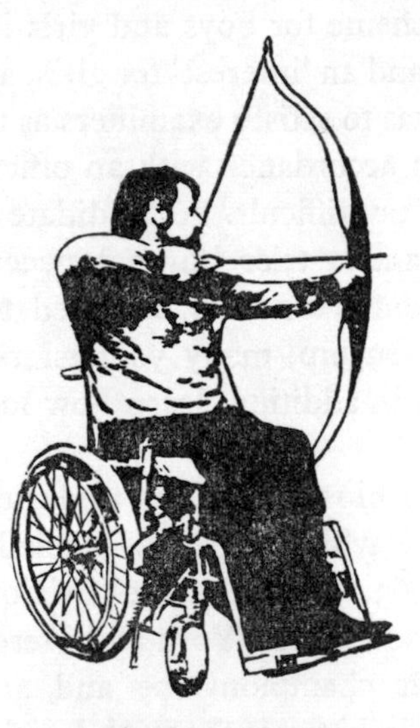

Fig. 10 A wheelchair archer taking part in the Paraplegic Games

tournament by their Rule of Shooting 103 (a) which reads: 'Shooting, except in the case of permanently or semi-permanently disabled archers, shall be from an unsupported standing position. . . .' This means that a wheelchair archer can take his place on the shooting line with his other more fortunate colleagues although he is not able to go to and from the targets unless he is wheeled there. It would be unfair to expect other archers to perform this considerable labour throughout a round and by Rule 105 (m) 'An incapacitated archer may nominate an assistant, who shall be under the control and discipline of the Judge or Field Captain, to record his score and pick up his arrows.' There are invariably plenty of willing volunteers to help out in this respect and often a small cork board, painted in target colours, is carried back and forth with suitable pins stuck in it to indicate the positions of the arrows in the target. This enables the wheelchair archer, even though confined to the shooting line, to see exactly where his shots hit the target.

It is interesting to note that there is a substantial psychological gain, which in itself plays an important part in the rehabilitation programme, where a disabled archer discovers that in competing against able-bodied opponents he can frequently achieve a higher score.

Where the use of the lower limbs is lost it is necessary to develop the remaining usable muscles to compensate for the uselessness of others. Posture is of prime importance and this involves the ability to balance in a wheelchair—no simple matter when the lower extremities are useless. Naturally the particular form taken by the initial archery training together with physiotherapy treatment will depend on the precise type of injury.

One of the foremost hospitals dealing with the extremely valuable work of rehabilitation of the disabled is the National Spinal Injuries Centre at Stoke Mandeville. The Director of this centre, Dr. Guttman, instituted an annual archery competition, and the first meeting was held on the day the 1948 Olympic Games were opened in London. Those taking part were all patients at the hospital or residents of the Star and Garter Home at Richmond, who had served in the armed forces during the war. This inspiring meeting enables medically controlled paraplegics to compete in a series of sporting events each year, and from those original sixteen competitors (who included two women) the Games grew to full international status in 1952 and now takes in paraplegics from all over the world, more than fifty countries sending representatives. A hope frequently expressed is that the courage, prowess and comradeship of these competitors will bring encouragement to handicapped people everywhere and will awaken the community to its responsibilities towards the physically handicapped, not only in providing rehabilitation facilities but in reforming attitudes of prejudice. However, it is a comforting thought that with the help of archery these prejudices are rapidly declining, and a person, physically handicapped through no fault of his own, can take his place on the shooting line as an equal to his more mobile companions. There are, of course, problems to be overcome in matters of technique, and some adjustment of routine shooting procedures may have to be evolved with the help of qualified coaches. Standard equipment usually presents no problems, except in cases where specific disabilities necessitate some extra ingenuity in the modification of hand grips or accessories.

No matter what age or sex, or misfortune of disablement, no matter whether the archer shoots for high scores or just for fun, there are certain factors which are common to all. Many of the rules by which shooting is controlled are officially published, many of the methods of handling bows and arrows are readily available and free advice from fellow club members is always forthcoming.

The appeal of archery is not only centred in the wide diversity of persons who enjoy it in matters of age, sex, and disability, it also attracts a very wide cross-section of society, from professions of every kind, the artisan or the less skilled, those with leisure to spare and those of restricted means; and in this respect it reflects the social revolution of the last five or six decades. There are also a number of additional benefits which members of the archery fraternity seek out and pursue according to their particular bent. For example for those who wish to shoot with traditional longbows there is the British Longbow Society, or for those who wish to study the history and development of the bow in all its forms, membership is open to them of the Society of Archer-Antiquaries, and for enthusiasts of the modern crossbow there is the British Crossbow Society. The National Film Library provides films on hire of general interest, together with technical and instructional films, and finally there is a group of dedicated archers who direct their energies exclusively to the training and coaching of archers.

Coaching

Never before has the beginner in archery been so fortunate as now. Whereas in years gone by he relied on a friendly club member or perhaps referred to a limited number of text books for his instruction in the rudiments of archery, today the services of specially trained archery coaches are available. Archery is a pastime which calls for initial teachings which seem, to the newcomer at any rate, rather complex, and before the present coaching organization developed, the special needs of the beginner were satisfied, or went unsatisfied, according to the amount of energy and degree of enthusiasm of a volunteer who took on the task of teaching as and when he could spare the time from his own shooting. The shortcomings of this arrangement are reflected in a quotation from Roger Ascham's *Toxophilus*—'The want of proper instruction causes many to decline beginning to shoot, and more to leave off shooting, when they have begun'—and the value of proper coaching arrangements are obvious from improved performances, a better appreciation of the sport, and enlarged club membership rolls.

The G.N.A.S. Coaching Scheme was originally devised to cope with the post-war expansion of archery and it now caters for those archers who wish to train as coaches progressively for club, county and region. To co-ordinate these activities a number of coaching organizers are appointed. The services of archery coaches, which are quite voluntary, are normally available on request and instruction is given, usually to groups of archers, at the club's own ground, in addition to which short courses of a day or weekend are regularly arranged at convenient locations so that a greater number of archers can participate. If a club has amongst its members an archer keen enough to become a club coach then, of course, instructing new members or brushing up the performance of those already shooting presents no problems. Some people have the knack of imparting knowledge to others and like to take on this valuable work, and for this specialized activity it is most desirable to have not only a thorough grounding in theory but also a reasonable proficiency in the sport.

The National Coaching Organization sets a number of progressive examinations, and archers who seek coaching status must first qualify as Instructors. This provides the necessary training for teaching beginners in clubs. After a two-year period an Instructor can then qualify as a County Coach, when his activities are widened under the direction of a County Coaching Organizer. A County Coach who serves for a further three years, after the appropriate examination, can then become elevated to Regional Coach, and when he or she has operated successfully on this level for a further three years he or she may be selected to become a Senior Coach. By this system the sport is assured of a group of dedicated coaches who have had wide experience and are able to provide a first-class voluntary service of training archers at all levels. New clubs can benefit from visits from coaches, members of established clubs can attend coaching courses to improve their shooting, and improved methods of shooting and training are passed on as a result of regular conferences and assemblies.

The National Association of Archery Coaches has been formed which promulgates information to its members, such as up-to-date methods of instruction and standard forms of teaching; it keeps a register of coaches, arranges courses and examines theories and techniques appertaining to the function of an archery coach. Such an organization is of additional value when specialists are required for examining boards, technical committees and as consultants, and it is also useful to be able to call upon members of this association to act as officials at tournaments.

3 · Variety in Archery

Target Archery

Target Archery as we know it today has descended from several other forms of archery practice, all of which developed as a result of the laws of the land directing that men should regularly shoot with a bow in order that a supply of trained archers should be immediately available in times of war. One very popular form of competitive archery was Butt Shooting which continued into the early nineteenth century. The butts were carefully constructed of closely packed turves in the form of a wedge and measuring about 7 feet high by 4 feet thick and some 9 feet wide at the base, this tapered towards the top where turves ornamentally cut in the shape of urns were placed. Upon these butts were placed circular pieces of thin white pasteboard, 4 inches in diameter. The winner was the archer getting the best seven arrows and no scores were recorded, only those arrows which landed within an agreed distance of the white disc counted, the distances varying according to the distance shot. To save trouble of constant measuring these distances the white mark was often placed on a larger blue disc of the correct measurement and eventually on a sixteen-inch disc (the size for 120 yards) with appropriate rings for shorter distances—12 inches for 90 yards, 8 inches for 60, and 4 inches for 30,[1] and shooting at this mark became known as 'shooting the inches' or 'the paper game'. Usually an equal number of arrows were shot at each distance, but only two at

[1] These sizes varied according to the taste of individual societies.

each end, and only hits completely inside the appropriate circle scored (1 point each).

The first mention of a coloured target very similar in pattern to those used today appears in 1754, when the stewards of the Finsbury Archers were directed 'to provide a target, or square pasteboard, covered with cloth; round the centre of which should be drawn a circle, and about that circle, four concentric rings, to be visible and exactly distinguished by colours'. The scoring values of the target in regular use were said to have been devised by the Prince Regent, who became patron of several societies of bowmen and helped considerably to popularize the great revival of archery. 'The Prince's Reckoning' laid down that a hit in the Gold scored 9 points, the Red 7, the Blue (originally the Inner White) 5, the Black 3, and White 1. It is also at this period that regulations were drawn up allowing for a set number of arrows shot at specified distances to be called a Round, the basis of all practice and competitive shooting today.

Present day Target Archery has changed little from the routine

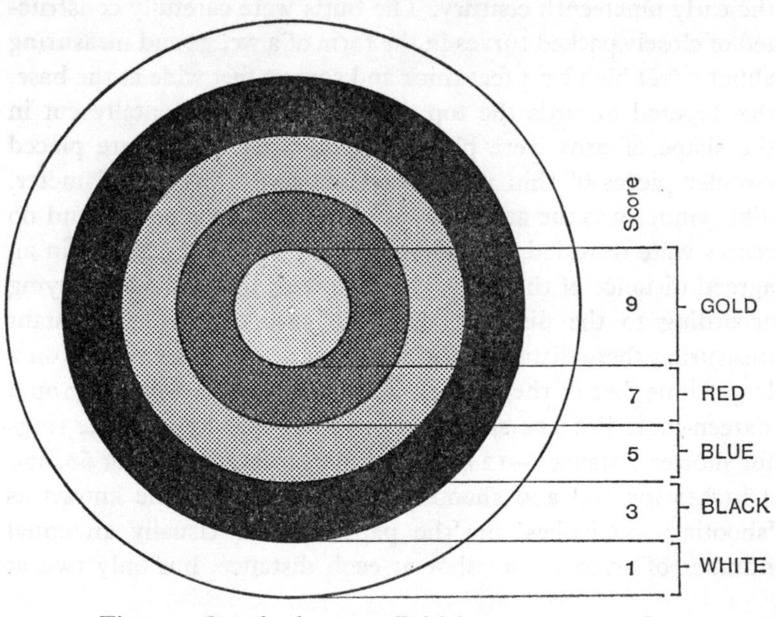

Fig. 11 Standard 5-zone British 122 cm target face

finally evolved in the early nineteenth century. Perhaps the only major change is that which occurred in 1949, when 'two-way' shooting was abandoned in favour of one-way. Before this

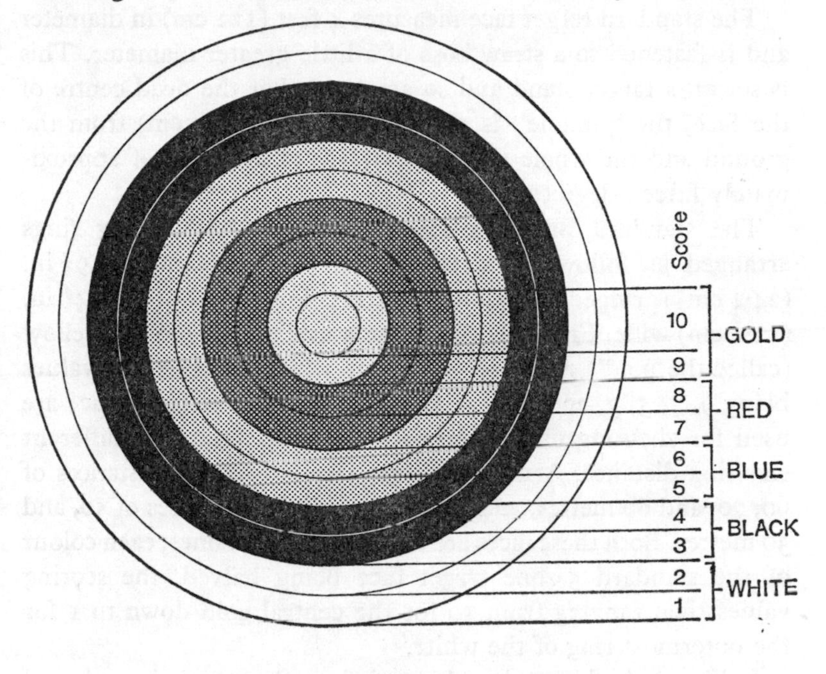

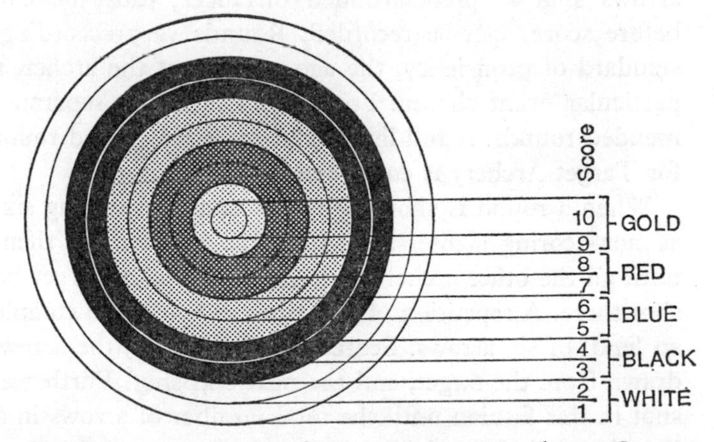

Fig. 12 F.I.T.A. 10-zone target faces; upper, 122 cm, lower, 80 cm

contestants would shoot from alternate ends at targets arranged facing in pairs. Today there are one shooting line and one line of targets.

The standard target face measures 4 feet (122 cm) in diameter and is fastened to a straw boss of a little greater diameter. This is set on a target stand and so arranged that the dead centre of the face, the 'pinhole', is about 4 feet 3 in. (130 cm) from the ground and the whole tilted backwards at an angle of approximately fifteen degrees.

The standard British 5-zone target face has scoring rings arranged as follows: a circle in the centre measuring $9\frac{3}{5}$ in. (24·4 cm) is ringed by four concentric coloured bands each $4\frac{4}{5}$ in. (12·2 cm) wide. From the centre outwards the colours are yellow (called the 'gold'), red, blue, black, and white; their scoring values being 9, 7, 5, 3, and 1 respectively. Two sizes of target face are used for shooting under international rules, each at a different shooting distance. A 122-cm target face is used for distances of 90, 70, and 60 metres, and an 80-cm face for distances of 50, and 30 metres. Both these faces are divided into ten zones, each colour of the standard 5-zone target face being halved, the scoring values then ranging from 10 for the central gold down to 1 for the outermost ring of the white.

In Target Archery a round, consisting of a specified number of arrows shot at predetermined distances, must be completed before scores can be recorded. Rounds vary according to the standard of proficiency, the age and sex of the archer, and the particular event chosen. For juniors there are separate recommended rounds. A full list of currently recognized rounds used for Target Archery is contained in Appendix A.

When a round is shot, each archer, after shooting six arrows as non-scoring sighters, shoots three arrows and then retires until all the other archers shooting at the same target have also shot three. A repetition of this process marks the completion of an 'end' of six arrows. Scores are then taken, the arrows withdrawn from the target, and the next end shot. Further ends are shot in this fashion until the total number of arrows in a round have been discharged.

Competitive Target Archery is regularly organized on the basis of friendly matches between clubs, in postal tournaments, and on a more serious level at county, regional, national, and international championship meetings. The *Rules of Shooting* published by the Grand National Archery Society, the governing body for archery in the United Kingdom, includes all the rules for Target Archery, regulations for championship meetings, and details of various other forms of archery.

Archery is generally a seasonal sport, that is when shooting takes place entirely outdoors, usually from early April until October. The long winter months when the bow is set aside can often result in the discovery of other pursuits, and regretfully some memberships are lost through a lack of continuity of shooting through this period. That is why many clubs organize indoor winter shooting, when the skills perfected during the summer can be kept up in readiness for the next season. There are added advantages in the fact that as members continue to meet regularly the club keeps its members during the out-of-season months. Regulations for Indoor Archery have been devised by G.N.A.S., with special rounds and a National Indoor Championship Meeting held annually. Generally speaking the rules for Target Archery apply with some slight modifications. Indoor shooting of another kind was introduced into the United Kingdom in 1964, when an indoor range was opened at Preston, advertised as 'Europe's First Automated Range'. The range had a series of lanes at the far end of which were arranged the standard archery targets each of which was mounted on a trolley. After an end of six arrows had been shot, the trolley with target and all, glides to the archer when he touches a switch. This innovation did not become as popular in this country as it was hoped, although in the United States it has been enthusiastically supported for several years.

Archery Darts

Archery Darts can be played indoors, and often matches are arranged with regular darts players. For this pastime standard faces can be obtained from archery dealers. These are merely enlargements of the patterns found on ordinary dart boards, and the shooting procedure is similar to playing darts.

Clout Shooting

This traditional form of shooting was well known by Shakespeare. In *Henry IV, Part II,* we find 'Shallow' commenting on the death of old 'Double'—

> *'Jesu, Jesu, dead!*
> *'A drew a good bow; and dead?*
> *'A shot a fine shoot. John a Gaunt loved him well, and betted much money on his head. Dead?*
> *'A would have clapped i' th' clout at twelve score; and carried you a forehand shaft a fourteen and fourteen and a half, that it would have done a man's heart good to see.'*

The distances shot are measured by the 'score' of yards and today are usually 9 score—180 yards—for men, and 140 yards or 7 score for ladies. To reach these distances arrows are aimed high in the air using their full trajectory to find the target. A mark on the lower limb of the bow is used and when the sight is taken in this fashion, beneath the hand, an arrow shot in this way is known as an underhand shaft. When the sight is taken above the hand the arrow becomes a forehand shaft.

The Clout was originally a small target boss marked with a black spot on a white ground and having a peg in the centre and was erected at a low angle in the centre of a target marked out in rings on the ground. This has been replaced in recent years by a flag. Having an outside diameter of 24 feet and five scoring areas defined by rings at radii of 18 in., 3 feet, 6 feet, 9 feet, and 12 feet the scoring values of the target are 5, 4, 3, 2, and 1 respectively, by ancient custom designated 'a foot', 'half a bow', 'a bow', 'a bow and a half' and 'two bows'.

Traditional Clout Shooting survives in its original form and is practised by the Woodmen of Arden on their lovely ground at Meriden and by the Royal Company of Archers in Edinburgh. Together with the more recently formed British Longbow Society they persist in the use of traditional longbows and wooden arrows, thus keeping alive this venerable pastime in its proper form. Many clubs include Clout Shoots in their fixture lists and often a pleasant day of target shooting can be rounded off with a Clout. Standard equipment can be used, although a set of light, barrelled arrows is often reserved for this purpose and a variation in the loosing technique—termed a 'snatch' or 'slip' loose—is usually employed, with the intention of getting the last ounce of energy out of a bow; this particularly applies to wooden bows.

Field Archery

This has become a very popular alternative to Target Archery, so much so that three separate bodies devoted to this specialized mode of shooting have been formed, catering for those who wish to concentrate on this form of shooting. They are: the English Field Archery Association, the National Field Archery Society, and the Scottish Field Archery Society.

Field Archery can be described, in brief, as practice for hunting under conditions actually resembling those met with in the field. Tough footwear, substantial clothing and appropriate weather-proof accessories comprise the standard rigout of a field archer; and a more powerful bow, to give a flatter trajectory, plus arrows fitted with 'field' piles are essential to compete successfully in this form of shooting.

In this urbanized island suitable ground for Field Archery is not plentiful, but ideally the terrain should be quite varied: trees and bushes, some hillocks, a lake, pond or even small stream in an area of about 10 to 12 acres would be needed for a full course. Targets consist of bold black and white circles or bold animal figures superimposed upon which are the scoring rings. These faces, which may be coloured to add realism, are fastened to straw bales or other suitable backstops and set up in positions as varied and as ingenious as the organizers can devise. The technique of shooting generally employed is termed 'instinctive' and the archer becomes proficient by adopting a stance quite unsuited for any other form of archery. An imaginary point-of-

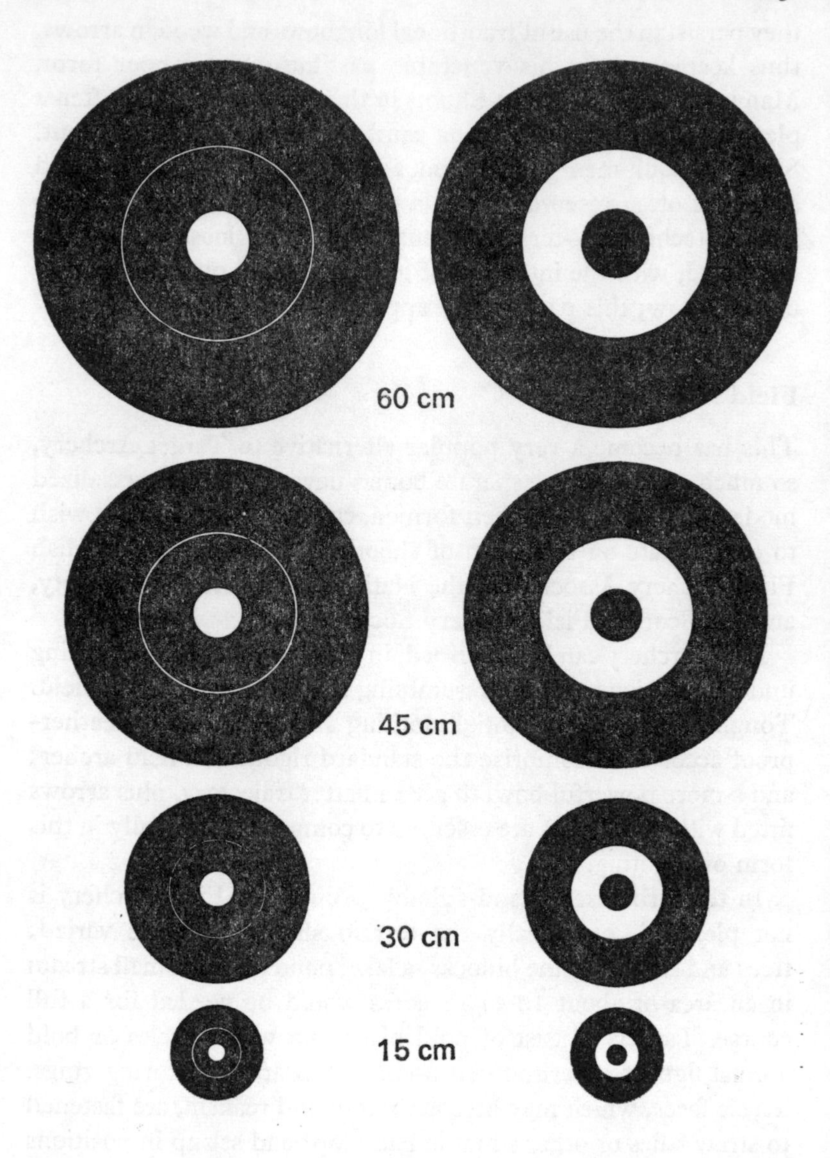

Fig. 13 F.I.T.A. Field Round standard circular target faces

aim is used, and experience in judging distance and estimating aim off is indispensable, together with a familiarity with the reduced degree of error that could be expected from a flat trajectory, all requiring appropriate training and the application of distinct theories inapplicable to Target Archery.

As in other forms of archery, special rounds have been devised for Field Archery, and various classes of competition are arranged with variations according to the archer's choice. The use of bows without sighting devices are included in the 'barebow' class. The 'traditional' class entrants use arrows made of wood, bow-sights can be used in the 'freestyle' class together with a choice of shooting of any of the field rounds either in marked or unmarked distances. For this form of shooting there is an All British and Open Field Championship, and similar competitions are held in other countries.

Flight Shooting

The highly specialized pursuit of shooting arrows with the sole object of reaching great distances has few adherents, but every archer is well versed in the highlights of the interesting history of Flight Shooting. It is a curious fact that this form of shooting is historically limited to the Near East and, quite surprisingly, Tahiti. Shooting for distance in Turkey is very well documented but our knowledge of this activity in the South Seas is nearly confined to the report of Captain Cook's voyages in those regions and specimens of flight arrows he brought home with him in the 1770s. As late as 1797 the Turks had detachments of archers in their armies, upon the purely conservative principle of avoiding a deviation from an ancient custom; for, in fact, archery had for years past been looked upon in Turkey as entirely an exercise of amusement, and as such it was at that period practised by all ranks of people. The principal activity which took place on the '*ok meidan*', or shooting field, was shooting for distance with richly finished masterpieces of the bowyers' art—the famous Turkish composite bow and finely matched, ivory-tipped arrows, slender and fragile shafts which are today as true as they were 100 or more years ago.

The bow, instead of being drawn with three fingers on the string, was drawn by the right thumb with the arrow placed on the string immediately above it. A thumb-ring, or guard, of horn or a similar hard material was worn. It was slipped over the joint and covered the ball of the thumb having on the inside a projecting tongue lined with leather. The index finger locked the thumb in position until the moment of release. A curious contrivance, called a 'sipur', consisting of a horn groove several inches in length fixed on a foundation of wood attached to a leather strap and buckle, was fastened on to the bow hand. The groove projected inwards. The arrow was laid in this groove and drawn back beyond the bow to a greater distance than it could have been without this device. Mastering the technique of the thumb lock is not easy and modern flight shooters use alternative methods of release which vary from flight 'hooks' to 'flip' releases.

The distances shot in the past were truly remarkable and many records exist giving us examples of the prowess of the Turkish master bowmen. The longest distance on record was shot in 1798 by the Sultan Selim who is said to have shot an arrow which drove into the ground at 972 yards.

Modern British records date from 7th July 1905 when Sir R. Payne-Gallwey shot a distance of 367 yards using a Turkish bow and arrows. The archery meeting on 26th June 1914, at Le Touquet, became historic when the late Ingo Simon achieved the splendid distance of over 462 yards. This remained a record until broken by Jack Flinton in 1953, at Oxford, with a distance of 482 yards. This was increased in 1974 by A. Webster to 695 yards. American flight shots have reached distances in excess of this figure.

Modern flight equipment is the result of careful study of ancient composite bow construction and the application of modern materials and advanced technological 'know-how'. It involves the use of a short and powerful bow, shooting slender lightweight arrows of special design. There are three classes in which competition may take place; the 'Target Bow' class, in which standard target equipment is used; the 'Flight Bow' class, which is reserved for competitors using specially made equip-

Fig. 14 Shooting in the Flight Bow class. Note the technique and stance which is unique for Flight Shooting

ment; and a 'Free Style' class, in which any form of shooting is allowed. As an example of thc incredible distances which can be achieved in Flight Archery, Harry Drake, in a Free Style class and using a footbow, shot a distance of 1 mile, 101 yards, 1 foot, 9 inches, in 1970. Flight Archery is an exacting form of archery but extremely satisfying, and, because flight equipment has to be almost made to measure, a challenge to the amateur engineer-craftsman.

Popinjay Shooting

The English word 'popinjay' is a corruption of 'papegai', the old French name for parrot. This name has been given to one of the most ancient of archery diversions which quite probably had its origin in the practice of shooting at a stuffed bird set high on the topmost parapet of a church tower. Medieval archers, as an alternative to butt practice, matched their skill in this unusual mode of shooting, exciting, no doubt, to the contestants, and hazardous, as it must have been, for the passerby.

In the sixteenth and seventeenth centuries the arrangements became much more elaborate—in particular on the continent—and many of the traditional companies of crossbowmen included Popinjay Shooting amongst their customary activities. In France and Belgium the Popinjay is still popular and blunt-headed arrows are used shot from normal bows. A mast 90 feet high is erected with a series of birds, made of wood decorated with coloured feathers, set on perches. These are known as 'cock' birds, 'hens', and 'chicks' according to their size, and when dislodged from their 'roost' score respectively 5, 3, or 1 points. The competitors stand close to the foot of the mast and shoot skywards almost perpendicularly.

Regrettably the Popinjay has not survived to the extent it might have done. No doubt the costly and elaborate arrangements required for the high mast, which can be raised and lowered as required, have helped to prohibit this form of archery in this country. However, one interesting survival of this ancient sport, in its original form, is to be found at Kilwinning in Scotland. Each year since 1688, apart from one longish break, the ancient custom of shooting at the popinjay—or 'papingo' as it is known locally—has been performed at the annual meeting of the Ancient Society of Kilwinning Archers. The bird, made to resemble a parrot, is constructed of wood, with wings which 'were made louse for shooting af' and which a slight touch could 'ding her doun', is set on the end of a pole some 100 feet up projecting from the top of the remaining tower of Kilwinning Abbey. Considerable skill is required to dislodge the 'bird', the successful archer being rewarded with the time-honoured title of 'Captain of the Papingo'.

Archery Golf

Sufficient evidence exists to refute the argument that golf was derived from archery. The Romans enjoyed a form of golf called 'paganica' and in the reign of Edward III the name 'camuca' was applied to this pastime; it would appear that the only connexion between the two games arises out of the early matches played between golfer and archer. A record exists of such a match played in 1828 at Musselburgh when Captain Hope, the archer, matched his skill with bow and arrows against a first-rate golfer with his clubs and ball. This novel idea consists of duplicating the tee shot of the golfer with a flight shot from a bow, for which a light-barrelled arrow similar to those used in Clout Shooting is best used. The golfer's approach shot—usually the most difficult from the archer's point of view—is matched by shooting a standard target arrow, and lastly the putting shot is duplicated when the archer holes out by shooting at a white disc of card 4 in. (10 cm) in diameter, placed flat on the ground level with the hole. On the green an arrow shot at very short range tends to skid and to avoid this a modified form of arrow pile is used, having a slender point 2 or 3 inches long, which will fix in the turf on impact. A normal target bow will serve admirably.

When the opportunity arises Archery Golf can provide novel variety for the club programme; it is a pleasant way of encouraging extra publicity and it invariably results in furthering good relationships and social activities locally.

Miscellaneous forms of archery

The variety of ways in which archery can be practised which have already been discussed are those for which rules have been drawn up by the Grand National Archery Society, and other authorities. A number of other forms of archery for which no official rules exist are described in the next few pages.

Rovers

Rovers, in common with Field Archery, is practised in rough country, the distances are unknown, and the same type of equipment can be used. But there the similarity ends. The original form of Rovers simply consisted of roving through the woods and fields picking out as a target any suitable mark, such as a log or mound. The archer who scored a hit or made the best shot chose the next object to be aimed at. As this sport became more popular it began to be played on a course with set marks such as existed over Finsbury Fields. These archery fields were lost with the encroachment of London's building development and are no more. Rovers is still occasionally played in its original form and no standard rules are used.

For centuries past archers have often amused themselves with aberrant forms of shooting and some of the more elaborate oriental archery stunts must have been spectacular as well as requiring great skill. For instance, imagine an archer on horseback galloping at full pelt and splitting arrows by shooting them at the edge of a sword, or shooting out the flame of a lamp, or at a hair suspending a small weight. Trick arrows have also been used for amusement over a long period and some of the writings of the experts of the past contain descriptions of some of these—which, however, are not always very clear. Shooting in the guise of light relief, as a complete change from the more regular routine of target shooting has always been welcomed by archers.

Under the heading of Novelty Shooting are listed those forms of archery which are mainly used for fêtes and Bank Holiday occasions when standard targets are replaced by unusual, amusing and sometimes bizarre marks at which arrows are aimed. It is sometimes good policy for a club to include a special annual Novelty Shoot in its programme and, depending on the facilities available, this can either be arranged by simply replacing the standard targets with novelty target faces or by planning an elaborate circuit of specially fabricated targets on which any amount of mechanical ingenuity and nonsense can be bestowed.

Different target faces can be easily devised such as coloured discs with scoring values; black and white stripes, the white to count and the black to cancel out a score; a humorous 'William Tell' face complete with apple, a bonus to be awarded if the apple is hit. Standard target faces can be used with hidden or reversed values of rings; a simulation of the Wand Shoot, in which aim is taken at a 2-inch wide lath set perpendicularly, can be arranged by sticking a tape of the correct width down the centre of the target.

Balloons are always popular and provide enough movement on a gusty day to test the skill of the club's best shots. Set on a pole, forming a modified Popinjay mast, they will provide extra novelty; but great care must be taken to plot the fall of the arrows beforehand, ensuring that they will drop into a safe area.

More elaborate targets can be used, involving moving targets, shooting through false medieval archers' slits, the use of a dummy with various features to be aimed at, a shooting gallery with 'plates' to be broken, flying objects, hanging targets and any conceivable arrangement offering something different. Apart from providing targets for Novelty Shoots different ways of shooting at these events can be specified which will often result in much merriment, such as standing on one foot, shooting from a recumbent position, using specially prepared out-of-true arrows, shooting left-handed when the archer normally shoots right-handed and many other unusual attitudes and postures which will confuse an archer's normal performance. Previous experiments must be carried out by the organizers of any Novelty Shoot to ensure that the competitors are not required to engage in impossible contortions and that the task they are asked to perform is within the realms of possibility.

Much more could be said about Novelty Shoots, but one essential that must not be forgotten is that any event scheduled as such must be properly recorded as a club fixture and care must be taken to ensure that proper safety precautions are observed.

4 · Learning to Shoot—1

The earlier chapters of this book have outlined much of the background knowledge of archery which is normally assimilated over a season or two. It is hoped that by now the essential basic technical facts about equipment which have been explained will enable the newcomer to handle bows and arrows as familiar objects. He, or she, will also have the knowledge that this sport has no bar to age, sex, inexperience or disability, and the confidence to approach fellow club members knowing that they will be like-minded. The diversity of activity, which can be enjoyed by archers, will have shown the beginner the wide choice open to him once he has mastered the elementary techniques of actual shooting.

At a conservative guess possibly half the knowledge of archery shooting techniques has been gained from manuals on the subject, a further twenty per cent by observing style on the shooting line and the remainder by direct instruction. The evolution of an individual style can be a mixture of all three sources of knowledge, but undoubtedly the most satisfactory method of self-instruction is by studying the teachings of acknowledged experts. Numerous treatises have been written on the art of shooting and briefly they fall into three classes:

1. Practical instruction manuals outlining the basic method of shooting, through which the student is taken step by step.
2. Advanced works on the finer points of technique with occasional technological information added for good measure.
3. Books describing highly specialized techniques and

methods of training involving theoretical profundities and styles inconsistent with regular practice.

In addition there are countless books, pamphlets and articles which concentrate on individual aspects of shooting.

It is apparent to the student archer that this matter could very quickly get completely out of hand and the individual could easily become bewildered by the unnecessarily complicated material thrust upon him by some teachers or be quite dissatisfied with the over-simplification by others. How can a standard work cater for those who are anxious to know all and yet at the same time be simple and informative enough for those who wish to apply only a few of its lessons ? The answer would be to present to the archer a wide selection of principal techniques, faults and cures, new conceptions and old theories together with many standard simple tips and then let him choose for himself. This is what is being attempted in this chapter.

One other important factor should be stressed, it is the contribution made by the National Coaching Organization, which includes a membership of dedicated individuals who provide a first-class voluntary service for the training of archers at all levels. Through the efforts of this organization a recommended Basic Method of shooting has been evolved, which provides excellent guidelines for the development of good shooting. The Basic Method represents the pattern of contemporary teaching of shooting techniques, and many of its principles are included in the notes that follow.

There is no short cut to expertise in archery but a lot of time can be saved by dispensing with those matters which do not suit your shooting and adopting those which fit into your particular pattern; when such an aspect of shooting in a bow is found, stick to it and practise, practise, practise.

Explanation of the method

In an attempt to offer in compact form aspects of good archery which can be compared and accepted or rejected by the individual, several authors of archery instruction manuals have been chosen and their interpretations of the same aspect of shooting set out in a manner for easy comparison. It should then be possible for the student to choose from the methods recommended by the different masters those which appear to suit the archer's own particular taste, combining them to build up an individual style.

The choice of masters presented few problems. It was felt that popular American methods and other teachings which are deliberate adaptations of oriental techniques or manuals which were merely rehashed from older standard works should be omitted. All these have their adherents and those interested in styles other than standard are recommended to search the quite considerable literature on the subject. Other excellent material, but again avoided for our purpose, deals with archery methods as applied to hunting and warfare. We are therefore left with a solid foundation of standard archery lore of British origin from which the following have been chosen as being most representative:

Toxophilus, the Schole of Shootinge Conteyned in Two Bookes by Roger Ascham, 1545.

Roger Ascham was born during the reign of Henry VIII, in 1515, at a village in Yorkshire, and became a noted English scholar and writer. His *Toxophilus* was presented as a specimen of a pure and correct English style, in the hope that the cultivation of the vernacular language by the scholars of the day would become as popular as the then exclusive study of Latin and Greek. In the summer of 1544 he wrote—'I have written and dedicated to the King's majesty a book, which is now in the press, "On the Art of Shooting", and in which I have shown how well it is fitted for Englishmen both at home and abroad, and how certain rules of the art may be laid down to ensure its being learnt thoroughly by all our fellow countrymen.' Although this work is not rigidly confined to the subject expressed by its title it does contain, among many other matters appertaining to shooting, the famous 'five pointes' of shooting—'Standyng, nocking, drawyng, holdyng and lowsyng', which 'done as they shoulde be done, make fayre shootynge.' It is these points that form the basis of our comparative studies.

Much of what Ascham wrote on the art of archery is as true today as it was when it was written over 400 years ago, and the principles he laid down, although then applicable to the longbow, are, with very little modification, of practical value to the modern archer.

Archery, its Theory and Practice by Horace A. Ford, 1856.

A clue to the value of this treatise is given by Ford himself in the Introduction, where he says that archery required 'both physical powers and mental study'. A second clue, revealing Ford's intellectual approach, is contained in his answer to a novice when he was asked 'Why don't I improve? I am always practising'—Ford replied: 'Ah that is the reason. You use your arms too much and your head too little; and so you go on repeating and confirming your faults, instead of mending them.' His shooting was the product of several years of intense study and resulted in his securing the British Championship for a total of twelve years, a remarkable feat of bowmanship which has never been equalled. His scores with the longbow a century ago have never been bettered and his career in archery can be considered to be quite the most outstanding both from the standards he set and the techniques he propounded. The method he perfected for his own use was based upon certain principles at once obvious and easy of application which are laid down in his treatise on archery. They consisted mainly in the recognition of the necessity of observing the ordinary laws of dynamics and vision. His approach was a fresh one and the result of logical and intelligent application of a series of simple principles to the art of shooting, regularizing the pattern and reducing the risk of inconsistency. Much can be gained from studying Horace Ford's *Theory and Practice* and the extracts that follow are selected with the present-day archer in mind.

An Archer's Notes, by C. B. Edwards, 1949. (Reprinted as Part 3 of *In Pursuit of Archery* by E. G. Heath and C. B. Edwards, 1962.)

'It seems to me that, when being taught the rudiments of shooting, the novice cannot appreciate why he is being urged to do certain things unless he has at the back of his mind those tiny details which add up to success, and which can only be fitted into a good style. I do not believe that a previous insight into the complexity of the problem of how to shoot well will scare him away from the attempt, but rather that it will make it easier for him to solve it. One must know what has to be done, before a successful effort can be made to do it.'

Thus Mr. Edwards introduces his *Notes*, and the subsequent pages reflect the many years of practical experience of this archer, British Champion and international shot of the immediate post-war years. Although basic principles of shooting do not change, the application of the finer details of those basic principles becomes progressively more complicated as equipment is developed to more critical standards.

So we have the basic method in Ascham's Five Points, Ford's logical and scientific approach, and the commonsense application by Edwards of how to shoot, to be studied at leisure with a view to selecting particular points suitable to be adopted as part of the archer's own individual style. Ascham is quoted only briefly, because, although his book is of enormous interest it is not essential for a novice to study it in detail. Extracts from Ford's treatise are given at some length because copies of it are rather scarce and his teachings should be most carefully studied and applied. Edwards's notes are readily available, so they have been quoted very briefly.

It must be emphasized that Ascham and Ford discussed shooting techniques which applied only to the traditional longbow of wood, and at the time Edwards wrote his book (1949) the only improvement was the introduction of steel bows, which have since become obsolete. During the past two decades or so the innovation of the composite bow has necessitated many variations in matters of technique. However, these changes are essentially additional to the basic principles which the three chosen authors took so much care to explain, and therefore much of what was written earlier is still valid.

However before these works are discussed the bow must be braced, or strung, ready for use.

Bracing a bow

The bracing height of a bow is the measurement taken at right-angles from the string to the belly of the bow; this varies according to the type and size of bow and can be anything from 5 to 9 inches. The bow must be braced according to the maker's specification and it is advisable to make a check at intervals during a day's shooting, adjusting where necessary. The bracing height of longbows was measured by extending the thumb and using its length plus the breadth of the palm as a rough and ready guide. The gauge so obtained was called a 'fistmele', but is quite unreliable for modern bows. The expression 'fistmele' is incorrect when used in reference to the bracing height of a bow.

There are two principal methods of bracing or stringing a bow, both of which are equally efficient and the choice rests with the individual. An alternative method can be used which involves the use of a special device. These by no means exhaust the variety of methods which can be employed: for instance the Asiatic bowmen of the past listed over one hundred variations—but for the purposes of modern archery those we describe will suffice.

The first method is most suitable for bows without recurved limbs, such as self wood or solid fibre-glass bows, but occasionally one finds the experienced archer using this method with a composite or a steel bow. Stand with the feet about a foot and a half apart and take the bow in the right hand about the grip. Place the end of the lower limb against the instep of the right foot, not on the ground, and cant the bow across the body with the belly, or concave side of the bow, to the left. One loop of the string should be in place on the lower nock and the other should be slipped over the top end of the bow and should rest loosely about 4 or 5 inches from the bow tip. Place the left hand, palm down, on the bow towards its upper end and take the loose loop between the fingers so that it can be easily slipped up the bow limb towards the nock. Now simultaneously pull with the right hand and push with the left; this will evenly bend the bow and the upper loop can be eased into position in its nock. Gently relax the tension and examine the braced bow to ensure that the

Fig. 15 Bracing a practice bow or a fibre-glass bow

string lies centrally along the axis of the bow and check the bracing height. The bow is now ready for shooting (see Fig. 15).

The second method of stringing is used extensively with re-curved bows which otherwise may be a little more difficult to manage. The string is placed in position on the lower nock, and with the feet some eighteen inches apart the hollow portion of the lower recurve is placed in front of the left ankle. The belly of the bow is now positioned behind the right leg and the bow handle is located against the back of the thigh. With the string held taut in the left hand and making sure that it is correctly in position on the lower nock, the upper end of the bow is now drawn forward against the back of the right thigh with the right hand. The upper loop of the string can now be slipped on its nock, the tension gradually relaxed, and bow examined for position of string and bracing height as before (see Fig. 16). However, this method must be used carefully to avoid twisting the bow limbs, and a safe and popular alternative method of bracing a composite bow is by

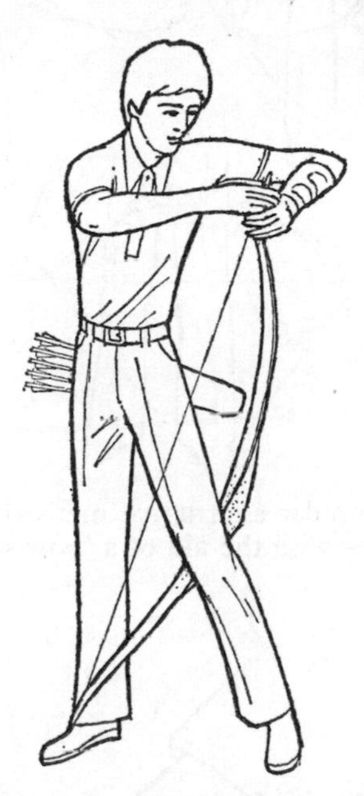

Fig. 16 One method of bracing a composite bow

using a bow stringer. This consists basically of an extra long string by which the bow is evenly flexed, enabling the bowstring proper to be placed in position (see Figs. 17 and 18).

Standing

Ascham: 'The fyrste poynte is when a man shoulde shote, to take suche footyng and standyng as shal be both cumlye to the eye and profytable to hys use, settyng hys countenaunce and al the other partes of hys bodye after a suche a behauiour and porte, that bothe al hys strengthe may be employed to hys owne moost a(d)uantage, and hys shoot made and handled to other mens pleasure and delyte. A man must no go to hastely to it, for that is rashneffe, nor yet make to much to do about it, for yat is curiosi-

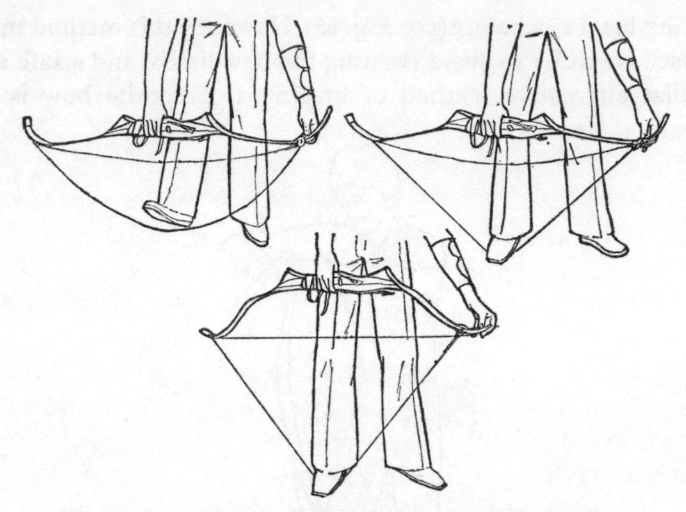

Fig. 17 A popular alternative method of bracing a composite bow with the aid of a 'bow stringer'

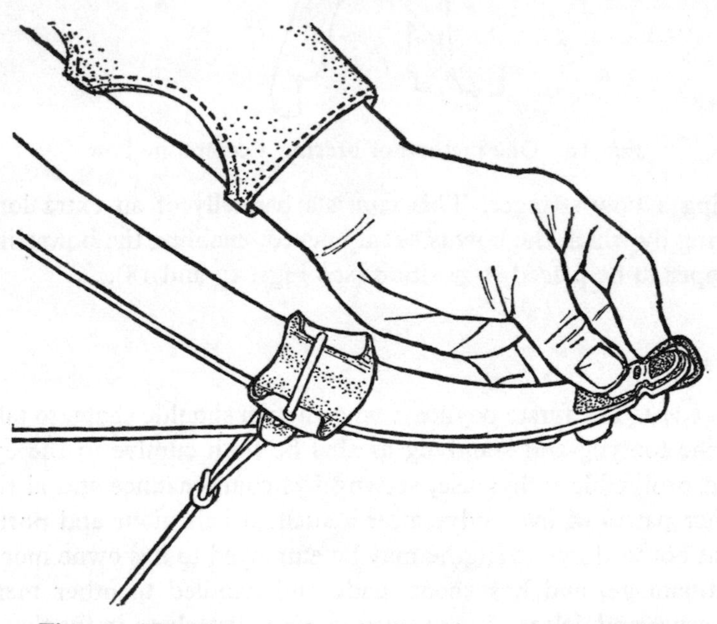

Fig. 18 How the string loop is slipped over the nock whilst the bow is flexed

tie, ye one fote must not stande to far from the other, leste he stoupe to muche whyche is vnsemelye, nor yet to nere together, leste he stande to streyght vp, for so a man shall neyther vse hys strengthe well, nor yet stande stedfastlye.

'The meane betwyxt bothe must be kept, a thing more pleasaunte to behoulde when it is done, than easie to be taught howe it shoulde be done.'

Ford: 'An archer's general position, to be a good one, must be possessed of three qualities—namely, firmness, elasticity, and grace: firmness, to resist the force, pressure, and recoil of the bow; for if there be any wavering or unsteadiness, the shot will probably prove a failure;—elasticity, to give free play to the muscles, and the needful command over them, which will not be the case should the position be too stiff;—and grace, to render the shooter and his performance an agreeable object to the eye of the spectator. It so far fortunately happens that the third requirement, namely that of grace, is almost the necessary consequent of the possession of the other two; for the best position for practical results is almost sure to be the most graceful one. At any rate, experience proves that an awkward and ungainly style of shooting is seldom or never successful. . . .

'The feet must be flat and firm on the ground, both equally inclining outwards from the heels, so that the toes be some six or seven inches wider apart than they; the position of the feet as regards the target being such, that a straight line drawn from it would intersect both heels—that is to say, the standing must be at right angles with the mark. The knees must be perfectly straight, not bent in the slightest degree. . . . The weight of the body should be thrown equally on both legs; for . . . a partial bearing on one leg more than on the other, tends to render the shooter unsteady, and enervates his whole action. In short, the footing must be firm, yet at the same time easy and springy, and the more natural it be the more likely it is to possess these qualities. . . .

'The left shoulder must not, however, be additionally forced forward, set in a vice as it were, but allowed to maintain its natural position—otherwise the required element of elasticity will be lost. The body should be upright, but not stiff; the whole person well balanced; and the face turned round so as to be nearly fronting the target.'

Edwards: 'On going up to the shooting mark, the archer first of all places his feet in a slightly stand-at-ease position with the heels about 6 to 9 inches apart so that a line drawn through them would run straight for the target. Standing quite straight and upright, a line through the shoulders will now also point to the target. There is one exception to the rule of standing perfectly square to the target, and this is that, if for some reason (too stiff arrows or a strong side wind), the point of aim is considerably to one side of the straight, the stance should be in line with the point of aim and not with the target, otherwise there is a tendency for the body to turn towards the target instead of remaining on the line in which it is desired that the arrow should start its flight.'

Coaching notes

For the practice of Target Archery the archer should stand astride the shooting line, and at right angles to it, in an upright, comfortable, and relaxed position with his weight distributed evenly on both feet which should be a comfortable distance apart, the recommended distance being about the same width as the shoulders. He should ensure that his shoulders are in such a position that a straight line drawn through them is directed at the target or aiming mark. This can be checked simply. Look straight ahead with arms outstretched level with the shoulders and, with the left eye closed, turn the head to the left and look at the target. If you can see that your outstretched left arm, the bow arm, is pointing directly at the target, then all is well. If not then move the feet slightly until the right position has been established. It is worth while taking care to check this position each time you shoot until you are confident that you are standing correctly. The direction of a line drawn through the feet in relationship to the shoulder line is of minimal importance, so long as you stand in a relaxed and comfortable position. Once a satisfactory stance has been taken the position of each foot can be fixed by the use of foot markers, which can remain until the end of a practice session or round. It is important that the correct shooting position should remain static, that is to say that there is no move from it, and the same position should be adopted each time shooting takes place.

The over-all aim when shooting a bow, particularly in Target Shooting, is to achieve absolute consistency in position, movement, and timing for each individual shot. It is through a conscious effort to achieve consistency that the basis of good shooting is established. This is a precept which should be applied throughout the whole sequence of shooting; with practice many of the necessary preliminary aspects can be performed automatically, but even the best archers find that from time to time they have to critically review their style. A bad habit is hard to break; it is easier to get it right to begin with until it becomes second nature (see Fig. 19).

Nocking

Ascham: 'To nocke well is the easiest poynte of all, and there in is no cunninge, but onelye dylygente hede gyuyng, to set hys shafte neyther to hye nor to lowe, but euen streyght ouertwharte hys bowe, Vnconstante nockynge maketh a man lesse hys lengthe.

'And besydes that, yf the shafte hande be hye and the bowe hande lowe, or contrarie, bothe the bowe is in ieopardye of brekynge, and the shafte, yf it be lytle, wyll start: yf it be great it wyll hobble. Nocke the cocke fether vpward alwayes as I toude you when I described the fether. And be sure alwayes yat your stringe slip not out of the nocke, for then al is in ieopardye of breakynge.'

Ford: 'When the arrow is nocked and the footing taken, let the bow lie easily and lightly in the left hand, the wrist being turned neither inwards nor outwards, but allowed to remain in that position that nature intended for it; as the drawing of the bow commences, the grasp will intuitively tighten, and by the time

Fig. 19 The correct standing position

the arrow is drawn to the head, the position of hand and wrist will be such as to be easiest for the shooter, and best for the success of his shot.'

Edwards: 'The arrow is now nocked and the fingers placed on the string. In putting the fingers on the string, the wrist should be turned outwards and should not be held straight or allowed to turn inwards towards the body. In other words, the back of the hand should be pushed forward. As soon as the draw is started, the wrist will straighten and the fingers will turn the string very slightly towards the bow helping to keep the arrow on the bow-hand or rest. Most beginners are troubled with the annoying habit which the arrow seems to have of falling off the bow hand, but, if the draw is started with the back of the drawing hand pushed outwards, it will be avoided.

'After nocking, the shoulders are thrown back, one or two deep breaths taken, and the eyes are fixed on the point of aim or the target, on the gold if possible. The weight of the body should be evenly distributed on both feet, on heels and toes, neither leaning forwards nor backwards.'

Coaching notes

Today there are practised two principal methods of nocking an arrow.

(a) The bow is held horizontally in front of the body. An arrow is drawn from the quiver with the right hand, laid across the bow against the arrow rest and drawn carefully back, engaging the nock with the nocking point of the string (see Fig. 20).

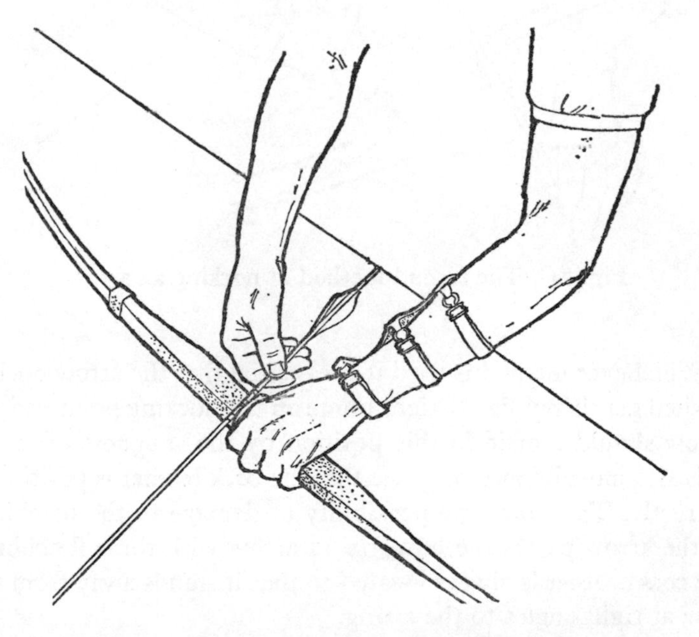

Fig. 20 The first method of nocking an arrow

(b) The bow is held obliquely across the front of the body with the string resting on the inside of the forearm. An arrow is drawn from the quiver with the right hand and held about half-way down the shaft, nock upwards. The arrow is then passed under the bow and the nock end is brought back towards the string and pushed home on the nocking point (see Fig. 21).

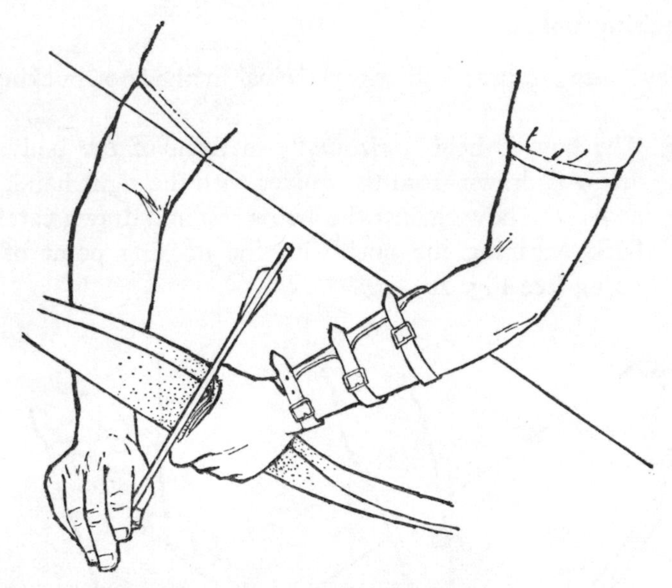

Fig. 21 The second method of nocking an arrow

Whichever method is used it is essential that the arrow nock is pushed gently but firmly right home on the nocking point and the arrow should remain in this position by the snugness of its fit. It is also most important to see that the cock feather is positioned correctly. To reduce the possibility of damage to the fletchings as the arrow passes the bow, on an arrow with three fletchings, the cock feather is always located so that it stands away from the bow at right angles to the string.

Each time an arrow is nocked it is possible to check that the bracing height remains constant if the cresting of the arrow is so arranged as to correspond with the correct distance of this bracing height.

The three fingers of the right hand, the shaft hand, are placed in position on the string, one above and two below the arrow. A correct initial position facilitates a smooth and steady draw. The string should lie across the crease of the first joints of the fingers and the forefinger should lightly touch the arrow. The hand must be flat and the wrist must be straight. When the bow is drawn the angle formed by thc string becomes more acute and there is a tendency for fingertips and arrow nock to become pinched together; apart from being painful this deflects the arrow on release, and to compensate for this a slight gap is allowed between arrow and fingers. It is recommended that about an eighth of an inch gap is left bctween the second finger and the arrow (see Fig. 22). Now gently take up the tension of the string, adjusting

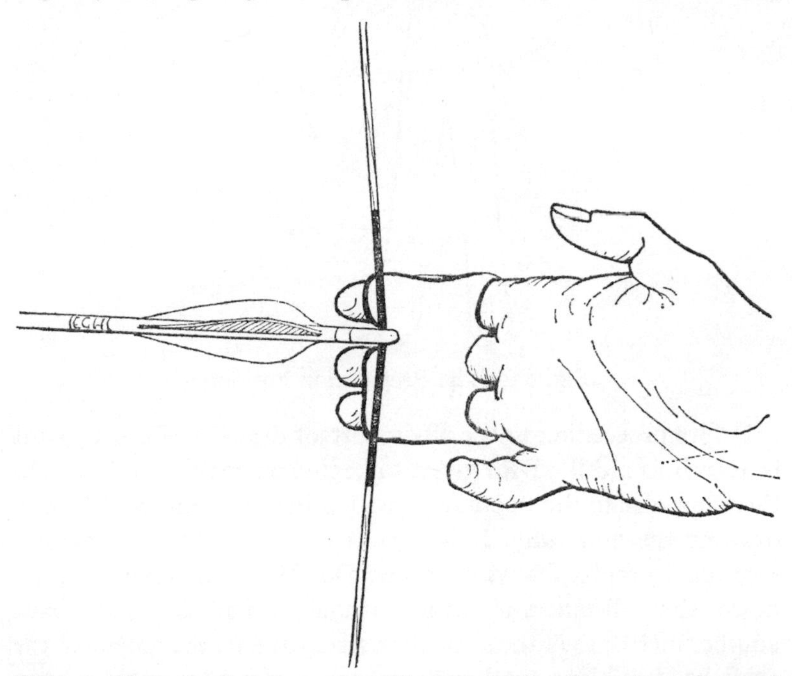

Fig. 22 How the fingers are placed on the string for a three-fingered loose

the final hand position whilst under slight tension. Keeping the fingers in place let the string go back to its normal position and check that the arrow and drawing arm are exactly in line, and remaining so throughout the sequence of shooting. This is known as the Preparation Line. When you are confident that everything so far is as it should be, clear your mind of extraneous thoughts, and with body poised, not tense, and above all comfortable, turn your head towards the target. You are now in what is described as the Preparation Position (see Fig. 23).

Fig. 23 The Preparation Position

Before proceeding to the all-important drawing of the arrow it is as well to recall advice given to beginners at this stage to help them appreciate the operation of shooting, without the effort of drawing the bow fully. It is a good idea to shoot a few arrows into the ground a few yards away. Do this by drawing back the bow a short distance, pause for a moment, and then draw back another inch or so at the same time straightening the fingers of the shaft hand. This is the loose, and when you have got the hang of it you will have some idea of the movement that is necessary to loose an arrow at full draw. Two simultaneous movements are involved; straightening the fingers and moving the hand backwards continuing the direction of the Preparation Line.

Drawing

Ascham: 'Drawynge well is the best parte of shootyng. Men in oulde tyme vsed other maner of drawynge than we do. They vsed to drawe low at the brest, to the ryght pap and no farther, and this to be trew is playne in Homer, where he descrybeth Pandarus shootynge.

'In shootynge at the pryckes [targets], hasty and quicke drawing is neyther sure nor yet cumlye. Therfore to drawe easely and vniformerly, that is for to saye not waggyng your hand, now vpwards, now downewarde, but alwayes after one fashion vntil you come to the rig or shouldering of ye head, is best both for profit and semelinesse.'

Ford: 'Whether Ascham's assertion that "drawing is the better part of shooting" be strictly correct or not, one thing is certain, that at any rate it forms one of its most important features; and upon the manner in which it is accomplished very much depends, not only the ease and grace of the entire performance, but the accuracy and certainty of the hitting. . . .

'I shall therefore venture to recommend, as being, all things considered, the best system of drawing, that the pulling of the bow and the extension of the left arm be a simultaneous movement; that this be to the extent of drawing the arrow at the least three-fourths of its length before the aim be taken (if to such a distance that the wrist of the right hand come to about the level of the chin, so much the better); that the aim be found by a direct movement on to it from the starting place of the draw; that the right elbow be well raised; and that the arrow be then pulled home either with or without a pause, preference being rather given to the latter.

'One of the main features of good drawing is, that the distance pulled be precisely the same every time, that is to say, the arrow always be drawn to identically the same spot. Unless this be accomplished, the elevation must be more or less uncertain, since the power taken out of the bow will, of course, be greater or less according to the extent it is pulled. . . .

'Finally, upon this point of drawing, it should be remarked, that the pull from end to end should be invariably even, quiet, and steady, without jerk or sudden movement of any kind.'

Edwards: 'This is best done with the two hands pushing and pulling respectively at the same time in a single steady motion, the bow hand arriving at its final position pointing at the aiming mark and the drawing hand at its anchor point simultaneously. The strain is much greater if the bow hand is poked right out first and the other arm is made to do the whole length of the draw starting from an awkward position far on the further side of the body. If the draw is made fairly quickly it will be less tiring than when made very slowly. It should, in fact, be done as quickly as possible short of being jerked. The best position for the drawing hand to start from is with the wrist in the middle of the body at waist height. There will be then no tendency for the rear shoulder or indeed the whole body to turn towards the target. The action is not performed solely with the fingers and the arms. It should feel as though the shoulders, right across the back, are doing the work and that they are using the arms and fingers as levers and hooks, until the shoulder blades come together. During the whole act of shooting, from the beginning of the draw until after the arrow is loosed, the breath is held with the lungs just normally filled, not after a specially deep breath.

'At this point, before going out on to the shooting ground, the beginner is strongly recommended to get the feel of the final pose at full draw with dummy equipment in front of a looking glass. If, aiming into the mirror, the reflection of the arrow is in one straight line with the arrow itself, things must be just about right. After this he should practise coming up, from the proper starting position, with or without an arrow hardly matters, not too quickly to the full draw, until he has really got the feel of it.

'There are a few points which we have not touched on in

connexion with drawing. The bow arm can either be brought straight to approximately the aiming position getting as near as possible on to the aiming mark right away, or it can be held up higher into the air and brought down, or it may be brought up from below. The first way is probably the best as it calls for the least adjustment of position at the end of the draw.'

Coaching notes

There are several ways in which the draw can be achieved. One method which is generally used is done with the two hands pushing and pulling respectively, extending the bow and string, at the same time bringing the bow to a vertical position with the bow arm fully extended, and drawing back the shaft arm until the first finger touches just beneath the jaw. The whole action

Fig. 24 First method of drawing, sometimes referred to as the 'push and pull' method

must be done smoothly and fairly smartly without jerking (see Fig. 24). A second method of drawing consists of raising the bow until the bow hand is approximately level with the top of the head, the upper part of the bow arm being in the full draw position. The shaft hand should be about six inches clear of the face with the nock of the arrow about level with the mouth. Bring the bow hand down, at the same time extending the bow to full draw (see Fig. 25). A third method of drawing starts with the

Fig. 25 Second method of drawing where the bow is brought down to the aiming position

bow held upright with the bow arm slightly bent. Draw back the string at the same time pushing the bow forward to full draw position (see Fig. 26). No matter what method of drawing is used, the final position that is assumed must be consistent.

The Preparation Line, which involves keeping arrow and shaft arm in a straight line, must be maintained throughout the draw

Fig. 26 Third method of drawing where the bow remains static and the arrow is drawn back to full draw

and in the final position at full draw. At full draw the string should just touch the centre of the nose and chin, and on no account must it touch the chest (see Fig. 27). This is the ideal and recommended arrangement and if there is any difficulty in getting this right a slight tilting forward of the head may be the answer. During the whole sequence of drawing no movement of the body should take place.

The anchor point is the position to which the forefinger of the shaft hand is drawn, underneath the centre of the chin, and it is to this point that the arrow must be drawn precisely each time a shot is made. To maintain the same distance between anchor point, string, and eye, is an important matter.

Drawing is the beginning of the sequence of shooting. From the moment the archer begins this movement there is only one escape from conscious errors. It happens, occasionally, that a

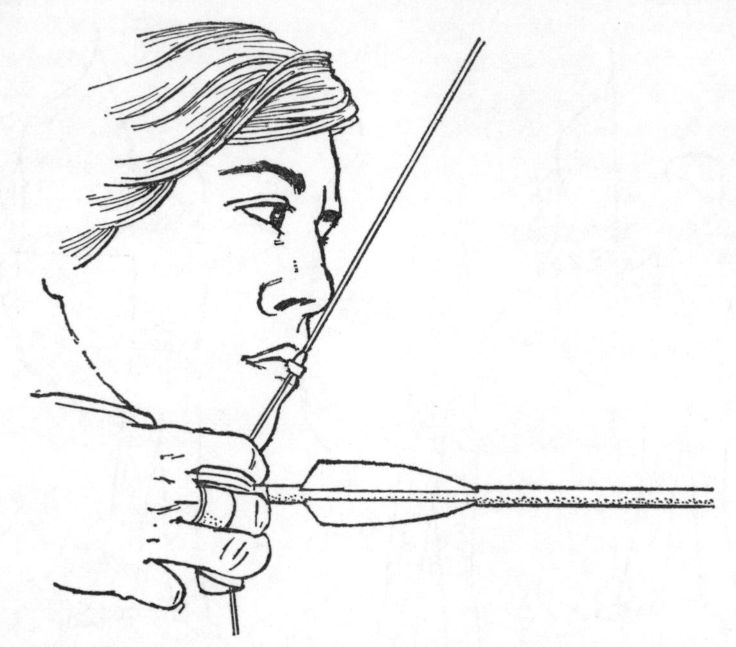

Fig. 27 This shows how the anchor point is achieved with the string touching chin and nose. In this example the archer is using a 'kisser' which helps maintain the correct string location

slight fault in drawing back the arrow, which could mar an otherwise perfect shot, is realized in time. Then the archer must let down his bow, replace the arrow in the quiver, take up the Preparation Position, clear his mind and start again.

Holding

Ascham: 'Holdynge must not be longe, for it bothe putteth a bowe in ieopardy, and also marreth a mans shoote, it must be so lytle yat it may be perceyued better in a mans mynde when it is done, than seene with a mans eyes when it is in doyng.'

Lord: 'During the brief period of time between the assumption of the footing and the loosing of the arrow, some slight alteration of the body's attitude first assumed will of necessity take place. During the act of drawing and aiming, the right shoulder will naturally come a little forward, and the left shoulder retire a little backwards. . . . The slighest possible inclination forward should also be given to the head and chest. The object of this is to bring the muscles of the chest into play to assist those of the arms, and is what good Bishop Latimer called "laying the body in the bow".'

Edwards: 'After reaching the full draw position there is a brief pause before the arrow is sent on its way. During this pause the aim is finally taken, all other vital points in the stance are checked over, bodily balance, pressure of fingers of both hands, position of elbows, anchor point, angle of bow and all the other hundred and one things which go into the making of a successful shot, but especially the length of draw. Getting the same length of draw every time is of such importance that a momentary distraction of the eye from the gold and from the sight just as the draw itself is completed is permissible. Enough time must be taken to get everything right and the archer soon acquires a regular rhythm, and everything possible should be done to stick to that rhythm. The whole mind must be concentrated on perfecting the aim and holding full length until the archer knows that he is steady on aim. It is best to bring the bow-hand up to the required elevation just before or at the moment the draw is completed, so that only a very small adjustment is needed after the shaft-hand has been firmly anchored. It will also be helpful to include in this final concentration a conscious feeling that the shaft-hand is pressing on to its anchor point.'

Coaching notes

This is the pause at full draw during which the aim is fixed, and it is also a convenient moment for the archer to make a rapid assessment of the correctness of every point which has to be observed to enable him to successfully accomplish the task ahead (see Fig. 28).

The many details which have been explained so far, if not done properly, will affect the final stages of the shooting sequence. It

Fig. 28 The aim being taken at full draw position

is at the moment of pause, when the bow is held fully drawn, that a number of faults may be recognized. It is much easier to see these faults in others, and to get someone, who knows what to look for of course, to watch your shooting can be a great advantage. Let us repeat the most important matters to watch for. The shaft arm and arrow must still be in line, remember the Preparation Line. The distance the arrow is drawn must be constant. This can only be achieved by reaching forward with the bow arm, slightly flexed remember, to exactly the same extent every time an arrow is drawn, and by drawing back the shaft arm to anchor at precisely the same spot. No movement forward or backward of either hand must be allowed.

The position of the arrow point in relationship to the eye must remain constant, both vertically and horizontally, do not tilt the head sideways. Any vertical alteration in the distance between the eye and the position of the anchor point, even a fraction of an inch, will be multiplied by the time the arrow reaches its destination. Pay attention to both hands. They should be balanced, that is to say they must not be twisted in relation to each other. The shaft hand should remain flat, the fingers should be straight and not slanted. Make sure that the pressure on the bow handle is evenly distributed and maintain this throughout shooting. Do not grip the bow too tightly. See that the bow is not canted to left or right, or tilted backwards or forwards.

Under no circumstances during this brief interval must the arms, chest, and shoulders be allowed to sag, producing the fault known as 'creeping'. In this the arrow imperceptibly creeps forward, thus shortening the effective draw length, which in turn reduces the power of the bow, resulting in a shot which falls short.

Many archers have experienced the irritation of the arrow falling off the arrow shelf once the bow has been drawn. This can be caused if the drawn arrow is pinched between the fingers, or if the shaft hand and bow hand are out of line or twisted in relationship with each other.

How long should the bow be held at full draw in the aiming position? This is a very personal matter, and the pause varies according to the archer. Some archers take what appears to be a considerable time before finally loosing the arrow, whereas others are brief. When shooting a round, under the rules of the Grand National Archery Society, a limit of two and a half minutes is allowed for an archer to shoot three arrows, from the time he steps on to the shooting line.

Loosing

Ascham: 'Lowsynge muste be so lytle yat it may be perceyued better in a mans mynde when it is done, than seene with a mans eyes when it is in doyng. So quycke and hard yat it be wyth oute all girdes, so softe and gentle that the shafte flye not as it were sente out of a bow case. The meane betwixte bothe, whyche is perfyte lowsynge is not so hard to be folowed in shootynge as it is to be descrybed in teachyng.'

Ford: 'After the bow is drawn up to its proper extent, and the aim correctly taken, there still remains one "point" for the archer to achieve successfully before he can ensure the correct and desired flight of his arrow to its mark; and this is the "point of loosing", which term is applied to the act of quitting or freeing the string from the fingers of the right hand, which retain it. It is the last of Ascham's celebrated "Quintette", and the crowning difficulty the archer has to overcome, in order to complete the perfection of his shot. Though the last point to be considered, it is not one whit the less important on that account; for however correct and perfect all the rest of the archer's performance may be, the result will infallibly prove a failure, and end in disappointment, should this said point of loosing not be also successfully mastered. . . .

'I think a great misapprehension exists amongst archers as to what is and what is not a good loose; it being generally thought that if an extreme sharpness of flight be communicated to the arrow, it is conclusive evidence as to the goodness. . . . Now without in the least undervaluing this very excellent quality in the flight of an arrow, and, *so far as it goes*, the goodness of the loose which produces it, I must still maintain that it is not the only requisite; and that unless a *certainty*, as well as a keenness of flight be also obtained, the archer's "beautiful loose" will be of little avail to him. Undoubtedly the best and most perfect quit of the string would be that which combines both of these qualities; but if the two cannot be obtained together, a slower flight and certainty rise immeasurably superior to the rapid flight and uncertainty: (of course it is meant as regards target, not distance, shooting).

'The question then resolves itself into this practical form: "Is it possible for the same mode of loosing to give extreme rapidity of flight, and, at the same time, certainty of line and elevation?" . . . This difficulty, amounting almost to an impossibility, of obtaining a loose which shall combine great sharpness and certainty of flight at the same time, arises from the fact that such a loose requires (to obtain that sharpness) that the fingers of the right hand be snatched from the string with such suddenness and rapidity as to compromise the second quality of certainty—such a sudden jerk of the string endangering the steadiness of the left arm at the final moment, and, by its unavoidable irregularity, not only having a tendency to drag the string, and, consequently, the arrow out of its proper and original line of flight, but also constantly to vary its elevation. Excepting for distance shooting, then, a *very* sharp loose is not to be recommended; nevertheless, in case he should be engaged therein, the *perfect* archer should have it under his command.

'It must not be supposed, from what has been said, that the exact opposite of the very sharp loose is advocated—that is to say, that the string should be allowed to slip, or loose itself, as it were, without any assistance whatever from the archer. On the contrary, this mode of quitting the string is the very worst that can be adopted, and one that does more to stay and unsteady the flight of the arrow than any other; in fact, no cast can be got out of a bow at all in this way. But there is a medium between the two extremes, and, leaning rather towards that of sharpness, which, in its practical results, I have invariable found to answer the best. The *modus operandi* like so many other things connected with archery, is extremely difficult to describe, if not altogether impossible; but the great characteristic with regard to it is, that the *fingers do not go forward one hair's breadth along with the string*, but their action be, as it were, *a continuance of the draw* rather than an independent movement, yet accompanied with just sufficient additional muscular action in a direction away from the bow, and simultaneous expansion of the fingers at the final instant of quitting the string, as to admit of its instantaneous freedom from all and each of them, at the same identical moment of time; for, should the string but leave one finger the minutest moment before its fellow, or all or any of them follow forward with it in the slightest degree, the loose will be bad, and the shot in all probability a failure. So slight is this muscular movement, that, though a distinct and appreciable fact to the mind of the shooter, it is hardly, if at all, perceptible to the looker-on; yet, though apparently of so slight a character, so important is it that the goodness of the loose, and the consequent accurate flight of the arrow, mainly depend upon it. . . .

'Especial care must be taken that, while loosing, the left arm maintains its position firmly and unwaveringly, and does not give way at the final moment in the slightest degree in a direction towards the right hand, as in this case the arrow is sure to drop short of the mark. It will have precisely the same injurious effect upon its flight, as would the allowing the fingers of the right hand to go forward with the string. . . . All must be firm to the last, and the attention of the shooter never be relaxed for a single instant until the arrow has actually left the bow.'

Edwards: 'Roughly speaking there are two types of loose: a dead loose and a sharp loose. The dead loose can best be described as a deliberate relaxing of the fingers, simply letting the string go when everything is ready. Inevitably the arrow will creep forward a fraction before it goes, it will fly in a heavy sort of way without life, but it will get there. The aim will have to be higher than it would be with a sharp loose, but this dead loose may be found to give good results at short distances. The sharp loose is got by an apparent, though not actual, feeling of increasing the pull of the fingers on the string until it suddenly and instantaneously slips off the fingers without any sign of creeping, or any feel that the fingers have been relaxed. There is another type of very sharp loose, which is not recommended because it is difficult to effect without a jerk. In it the arrow is not brought to a completely full draw, but is left with about half an inch or a bit less to spare while the aim and everything else is settled; then, when all is ready, it is pulled back very quickly and loosed all in one action. This gives a very fast flight, but is not very reliable for target work.

'At the moment of loosing, the natural reaction, which cannot and should not be prevented, is that the bow hand will go forward a little and the shaft hand come back a little, and provided they do this in the line of aim all will be well. The bow hand must be prevented from jerking away to one side; it must be resolutely held on the aiming mark. The shaft hand must remain all the time against the face.'

Coaching notes

Whereas with some application a beginner can soon get the hang of this action, the perfecting of a correct loosing movement is not easy to acquire and takes considerable practice. Archers are aware that the loose is the most critical of all the points of archery and extra effort in the management of finger movements in the early days will prove beneficial as the archer becomes more skilled. The action required is simple. Once the arrow, bow and string are positioned at full draw in exactly the right alignment towards the mark, all the stored energy must be suddenly released so that the bow can propel the arrow to its required destination. This works extremely well—if none of the positioning is disturbed. The string is held back by half-bent fingers in an unnatural tension, the bow is held forward in space to just the right distance and the eye is momentarily mesmerized by a good aim on the target. Alter one of these by a fraction and the shot is spoiled. There are many other minor considerations which, once settled, must not be altered. Imagine that the archer stands firm and that his fingers holding the string were suddenly not there and you have a reasonably good idea of the sought-after action of loosing (see Fig. 29).

The string must not gradually slip off the fingers neither must they be snatched off the string; the loose must be smooth and easy, without any jerk.

The recommended method of achieving a good loose consists of a series of carefully controlled simultaneous movements. The shaft arm, holding back the arrow, should be relaxed, and held in position by the back muscles. If a little extra muscular effort is exerted from the back this will result in the arm being moved slightly back, which results in the string being pressed back a little harder on to the chin. At the same moment the fingers holding the string should be straightened, and the arrow leaves the bow. These movements, which are hardly perceptible to the observer, must be exactly co-ordinated, and that being the case no change in string position results up to its final release, and the loose is clean and sharp.

Fig. 29 The loose and follow through position

The fingers should be relaxed and not stiff or taut when they are straightened, and it is most important that all three fingers should quit the string simultaneously.

Because of the released tension of the drawn bow the drawing hand will continue to move backwards, close to the neck. Often this backward movement is continued for an inch or so, or even further, and provided a clean loose is achieved there is no harm in this. However, it is important to keep the hand from turning, certainly not until after the loose has been completed. Wrist and hand are relaxed, and this relaxation will be apparent once the string is free of the fingers.

The tendency to allow the arrow to creep forward momentarily before the loose must be carefully controlled, remember that the arrow must remain exactly at the same drawn length until the actual moment of release.

5 · Learning to Shoot—2

The archer's vision

One essential and often neglected aspect of shooting is the part played by the vision of the archer. Without this faculty there would, of course, be no archery, and a full understanding of the importance of the optical functions and the accompanying problems of aiming will make all the difference between accurate shooting and inconsistency. When a sight is taken with an arrow at full draw both eyes can be open or the disengaged eye closed; in either case only one eye is used, the one known as the dominant or guiding eye. With very few exceptions everyone can quite easily check which is their dominant eye. Hold both hands out in front at arms' length and form a peephole with the thumbs and fingers, about $1\frac{1}{2}$ in. across, and look at a small distant object through the opening (see Fig. 30). Now, without moving

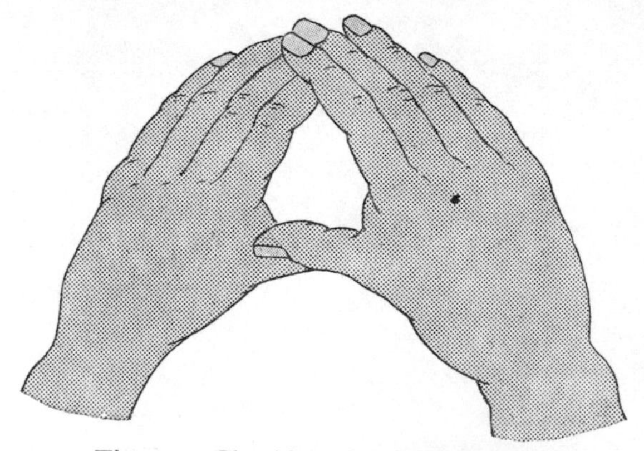

Fig. 30 Checking the dominant eye

your head, close one eye and then the other. Whichever eye still sees the distant object through the opening is your dominant eye. This eye, doing your sighting for you, is naturally of the utmost importance. A right-handed person (the bow held in the left hand) whose left eye is dominant is going to have some difficulty in shooting for the reason that because of the visual phenomenon which takes place (physiological diplopia) it is impossible to accurately line up sight, arrow and target, and any aiming corrections made will be offset by this optical falsity. If, of course, the archer is left-handed (the bow held in the right hand) there would be no problem, and for those who have difficulty in this respect it is worth while reversing the handling of the bow in the very early stages of shooting practice.

Provided the archer is aware of which eye is the dominant and shoots left or right-handed accordingly, it will also be found advantageous to practise shooting with both eyes open, this will enable the dominant eye to take over. It is possible to overcome eye dominancy by training the inferior eye to work, but this would depend on constant and concentrated practice of a specialized nature and is a subject outside the scope of this book.

In addition to the problem of eye dominancy, there are other visual factors to be considered. The eye is subject to defects in acuity such as hypermetropia (far-sightedness), myopia (near-sightedness) and astigmatism. These are only the more common refractive errors and are usually correctible with glasses.

Hunting with the bow is not within easy reach of archers in this country but a growing interest in Field Archery has been apparent over the last few years. Good vision is possibly even more important with this wider scope of archery, and several other optical factors can considerably reduce the standard of an otherwise excellent archer. For example one skill necessary for accurate Field Archery is good depth perception or, as far as we are concerned, the ability to judge distances. The extent to which you can see up and down and to the side while looking straight ahead is your visual field and utilizes peripheral vision. This field is used when leading (aiming off) at moving targets and it warns of approach from either side. You should be aware of any defects in your field of vision so that you can govern your shooting accordingly.

There are a surprisingly large number of people who are colour-blind. Accidents have been caused through not being aware of this defect and if you know your limitations in this respect greater safety will result.

Any defects, if not cared for, can undermine the archer's enthusiasm and a periodic check will result in benefits not only to his performance with the bow and arrow but also to his general well-being. The wearing of corrective lenses need not be a handicap to good archery, the only necessity being that they should be of the corrected curve type. They must have the same power at the edge of the lens as they do at the centre, as a sight is often taken off-centre through the lens. So many physiological and psychological aspects are closely linked and it has long been recognized that if the mind is clear of worry or tension higher standards of archery are more accessible and what is more the enjoyment is greater. Bad vision can be a worry, which can manifest itself in nervous tension, resulting in a poor performance disappointing to the student archer and unsatisfactory to his teacher. The importance of your eyes working properly for you cannot be over-emphasized and they must not be neglected.

Aiming

This subject is very often dealt with only briefly, and consequently many beginners are unable to understand fully the principles of aiming, with a result that they experience disappointment in their early efforts to hit the target without sufficient knowledge to correct what may be a simple error. This can lead to a dwindling interest in the sport and the possibility of a lost membership. It is all very well for a beginner, in the rudimentary stages of archery, to be told that it matters little whether the target be hit or not; this may well be so—in fact emphasis on correct stance, bow position, draw technique and loose is of primary importance in the early days—but there is no doubt of the value of the psychological encouragement of hitting a target, even at very short range. Therefore it is quite important that early lessons in theory should be devoted to aiming.

It is assumed that the arrows used are the correct length, weight and spine for the bow and that any discrepancies resulting from faults in technique are discounted. Generally speaking, except for a very short distance, an arrow does not travel in a straight line. As it loses speed it starts to fall in a low curve. This part of the the arrow's flight is called a Trajectory. The Line of Flight is the path the arrow takes when viewed from above, and this can be deflected from a straight line by wind variations. The course of the arrow has to be initially calculated so that it reaches home on the target. This initial calculation is the result of trial and error and is based on the fact that there are several constant factors by means of which the pattern of aiming is constructed (see Fig. 31). They comprise: the eye of the archer,

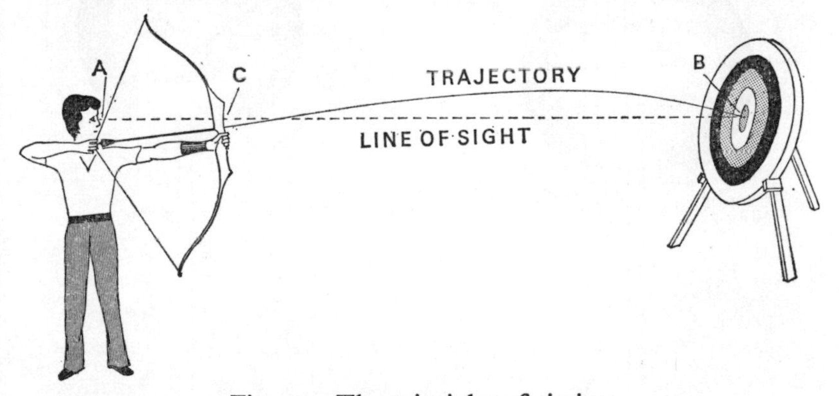

Fig. 31 The principles of aiming

'A', the target or aiming mark 'B', and the sighting mark 'C', (whether it be a mechanical sight or pile of the arrow). These, combined with the angle of elevation and Line of Direction of the arrow pivoted from a constant anchor point location, provide a reasonably accurate method of aiming a bow.

The ideal aiming arrangement occurs when the Line of Sight cuts the Trajectory of the arrow exactly at the pile of the arrow at full draw. The arrow pile can then be visually placed 'on the gold' which will be hit by the released arrow (see Fig. 32). Let us assume that this aim is taken and the arrow overshoots. Some adjustment has then to be made. It is clear that in this case the elevation of the arrow has to be depressed to enable the lesser distance to be reached. With all other positions remaining constant this will result in the view of the target appearing 'higher' in relationship to the arrow (see Fig. 33). If a mark is made on the

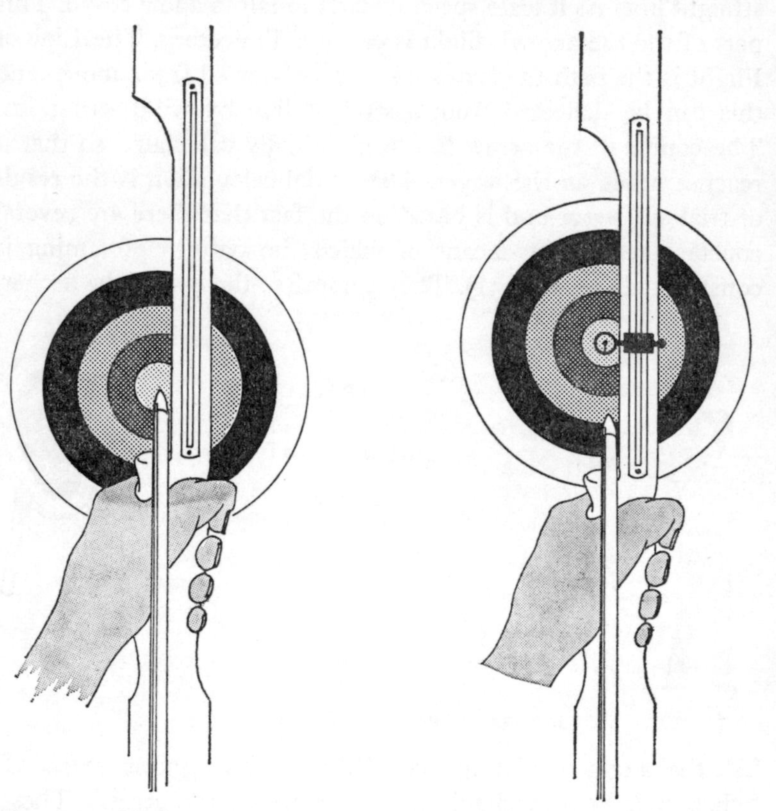

Fig. 32 Aiming with the pile of the arrow on the gold

Fig. 33 Aiming with a sighting device on the bow

bow limb it will be seen that this aiming position can be assumed time after time, and if an adjustable sighting device is fitted at this point an even more accurate control can be attained. This really performs the same function as a foresight on a rifle, but unlike that weapon a bow has no backsight. It is therefore important to remember that the angle of elevation of the arrow should be accurately controlled, any slight variation at one end or the other producing an enlarged error at the target. For instance, if the mouth is closed for one shot and for the next it is open, the jaw moving downwards depresses the nock end of the arrow half an inch or more, and although the aiming is the same an error is produced of possibly four feet at the target end.

Marks on the bow or positions on the sight slide for various distances can be established but they will vary slightly according to weather conditions. A following wind, blowing down the range towards the targets, will lift the arrow and extend its range, so the sight used will be a little higher than normal. Alternatively a head wind, from the targets, will depress and shorten the flight of an arrow, necessitating the use of a lower sighting mark. Cross winds may affect the line, and these have to be allowed for by aiming off into the wind. The degree of adjustment will depend on the strength of the wind and can only be judged by experiment and common sense.

The foregoing method of aiming is that most commonly used in Target Archery, but for other types of shooting there are alternative methods. The instinctive method is used when the distances being shot are unknown, as in Field Archery and hunting, and for this no mechanical sights are used. Various techniques are used, but basically this form of aiming relies on the use of a more powerful bow, with a much flatter trajectory, so that more control over the arrow elevation is obtainable and a visually assessed 'aim off' distance is used with considerable accuracy.

Freezing

The extreme accuracy of aim required for Target Archery necessitates a pause in the rhythm of shooting whilst the sight is lined up with the mark. This is held for varying periods whilst the archer makes certain that his stance, draw length, grip, aim, and many other factors are all as they should be. Various schools of teaching enumerate the order in which the list should be mentally checked, but however this is done the pause 'on aim' must be relaxed yet under control. Therefore, as it represents the accumulation of effort and mental concentration immediately before the moment of loose, this pause is vital.

When the arrow leaves the bow it is charged with energy and its direction is pre-determined—which conditions entirely depend on the climax of physical control on release. Thus any factor which interferes with the proper management of the pause should be thoroughly investigated and dealt with.

So long as the whole sequence is controlled by conscious effort no problems arise. Once the process of shooting starts to become an automatic order of events the eye is allowed to take over during the pause and a conditioned reflex develops, the muscular mechanism for releasing the arrow is tripped by the eye and the arrow is discharged prematurely. It is found that it is impossible to hold the sight on the gold and attempts to visually bring it in to position only produce a 'freezing' of the aim.

Much has been written about this malady and many theories have been advanced as to its cause and cure. It has been searchingly discussed by medical experts, dismissed casually and sometimes lightheartedly by victims and observers alike, and occasionally dismally accepted as inevitable and incurable. It has caught the attention of every modern writer on archery shooting techniques and has been variously called Target Shyness, Gold Shyness, Target Panic, Archer's Paralysis, Freezing, and many other descriptive and uncomplimentary names. The archer afflicted will find it all too easy to recognize, although the beginner can take heart as it seems to affect only those who have reached a reasonably proficient standard of shooting. Let us consider what causes this inability to hold the aim.

The process of reasoning by which psychologists explain the condition is profound; instead of discussing these complexities let us examine some of the practical factors which are known to encourage and aggravate the situation. These can be grouped as influences which interfere with the normal rhythm of shooting. This rhythm is quite an individual matter and has to be gradually evolved, for this reason a novice, not having produced such a pattern of his own, rarely experiences the freezing effect of these influences. The use of wrong muscular tensions through being over-bowed is a common factor, another is fatigue. The influence of anxiety or tension felt in competition, or worry over the next shot being a bad one, lack of adequate powers of concentration, distractions of various kinds—all these can contribute to the utter breakdown of the fractional moment between aiming and loosing. To summarily deal with the causes of this problem as we have done does not do justice to the enormous amount of analysis and study of it contributed by specialists of medicine and toxophily over the years. However, it is our intention to provide the means of recognition and, what will be more comforting, suggest a cure.

In the first place an archer who experiences 'freezing' for the first time must stop and decide on the course he must take—trying harder merely aggravates the problem. One thing he can be absolutely certain of is that the situation is not hopeless. Usually it is not enough to remove the cause, even if it has been identified as still being present; it is necessary to neutralize its effect. Much has been said about the rhythm of shooting which has been consciously achieved. It is the part of this rhythm, between aiming and loosing, which has become automatic which we are aiming to bring into line as part of the conscious performance. Alter this and the fault has been neutralized. Possibly the cure sounds too easy; there is no guaratee that it will be permanent, but as there are countless variations of change which can be applied any number of cures can be effected.

Any positive alteration will usually work: adopting a different form of shooting, using alternative methods of sighting, changing a bead sight to a ring sight, altering the sighting mark on the target to a spot other than the gold, using both eyes open instead of one, and—a drastic one—changing from right-handed shooting to left or vice versa. Some authorities advise the introduction of an intermediate stage of shooting between aiming and loosing described as 'balance', and many archers find the solution in the use of a 'clicker', which is a gadget to audibly indicate the moment when the arrow is fully drawn. Numerous other changes work equally well but it is important to persevere with whatever new arrangement is chosen, remembering that it is up to the archer concerned to make the change work for him as no alteration can automatically eliminate this very common malady.

Faults and remedies

The recognition of faults, their analysis and correction has occupied a great deal of space in the textbooks of archery over the years, and advice as to how one should approach the practical aspects of shooting invariably includes warnings of the pitfalls likely to be met. The beginner expects to make initial mistakes, though it is logical to assume that having the proper instruction and following it precisely should lead to the elimination of errors at the outset. However, it is rare for anyone to become so proficient that he is faultless, even with the up-to-date coaching methods used today. It is commonplace for a fault to develop quite suddenly and unbeknown to the archer even though he may have years of experience of first-class shooting to his credit. Some of the results of faulty performance are sadly too obvious to the archer and spectator alike, when for instance the shots miss the target completely; other manifestations of bad shooting are not so obvious and can bring disappointment and bewilderment to the shooter particularly when he is not aware of their cause.

Everyone on the shooting line at some time or other realizes that something is wrong, or feels that the rhythm of shooting is momentarily out of tune and is vaguely aware that he or she is doing something incorrectly. Quite often the feeling is dismissed and shooting continues, uninterrupted by any self-analysis, advice from others, or correction, very likely because time presses and the round must be finished, or perhaps because of the more homely fact that tea is almost ready. The damage has been done. A fault has crept in and if something is not done about it it will return and very soon it will begin to produce a deterioration in shooting. Far better to sacrifice the last dozen or so arrows in a round, or the first cup of tea, and devote a little time to the very necessary labours of fault correction. It is not a disagreeable task—in fact it becomes personally satisfying to identify the most insignificant fault, and an individual triumph when it is conquered. It is only by a deliberate and methodical process of deduction that one can identify just what is wrong.

A mental appraisal of all the things that should be done will often reveal the fault or it is sometimes helpful to persuade a friend to watch every movement and to point out the obvious mistakes. It is always easy to see certain defects in other people's shooting although the archer concerned may be oblivious of their presence. It is easier to pinpoint a fault if at least six arrows —one end—are considered and it is of little use isolating the performance of any one arrow. The better the arrows are grouped on the target the easier it is to correct their collective position and this applies, to a large extent, if the arrows are in a good group on the ground.

The four basic results of inaccurate shooting are:

1. Shooting high on the target or over.
2. Shooting low on the target or short.
3. Shooting to the right or missing right.
4. Shooting to the left or missing left.

The following permutations can be added to the above:

High-right, low-right, low-left, and high-left.

These can be termed consistent errors which usually result from bad technique and sometimes a combination of several faults, each of which must be found and corrected.

Now follows a guide to some of the most common faults in technique which are responsible for the four basic errors.

1. *Arrows high*

This can result from over-drawing, which in turn may be due to bad stance, the re-location of the anchor point to a position further back on the jaw or using arrows which are too long. It could also be caused by dropping the shaft hand, or opening the mouth when it is normally closed—which will have the same effect, or alternatively lifting the bow hand. On the loose a push forward of the bow will result in arrows flying high as will a loose sharpened or snatched in an inconsistent manner.

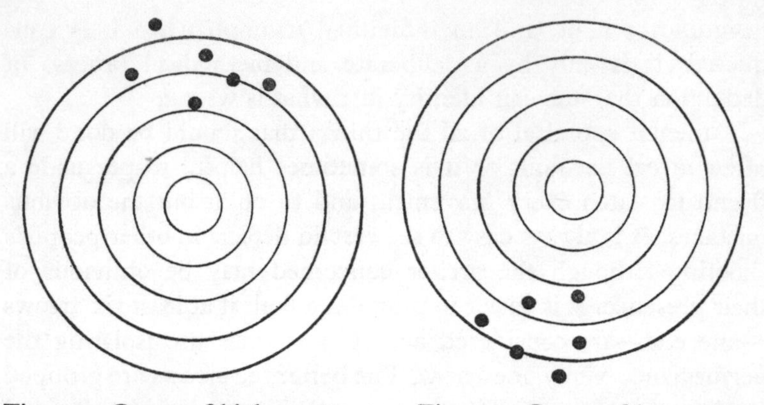

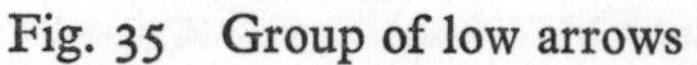

Fig. 34 Group of high arrows Fig. 35 Group of low arrows

2. *Arrows low*

Commonly caused through under-drawing, resulting from allowing the arrow to creep forward before the loose, a bow arm which imperceptibly sags or collapses or holding the aim too long. Can also be caused through dropping the bow hand on release or a sluggish loose.

In the case of arrows flying high or low it is worth while carefully checking the sighting device to see that it is correctly positioned. Also the bracing height should be seen to, as this can seriously alter the cast of the bow if it is not set at the specified distance.

3. *Arrows right*

This is often caused by jerking the bow hand to the right on release, a slackened grip on the bow or too much torque in gripping the bow. Possibly the string is held too deeply on the fingers or the fingers are not opened cleanly enough on release.

4. *Arrows left*

In this case the grip on the bow can be too tight or excessive torque is being applied in the opposite direction. Possibly the anchor point is too far right or the bow is strung too low. A common fault is allowing the shaft hand to jerk away from the

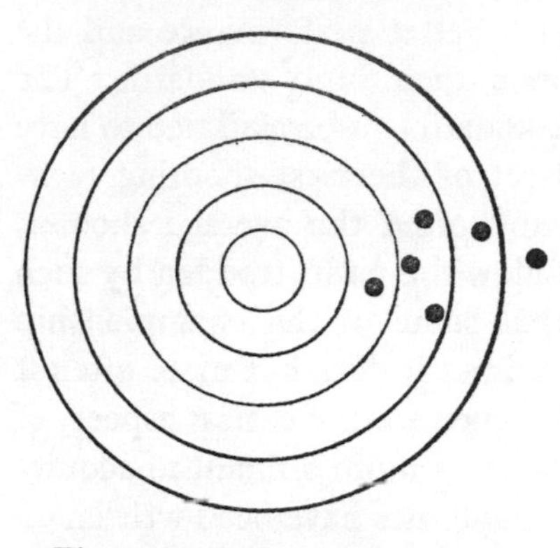

Fig. 36 Group of arrows to the right

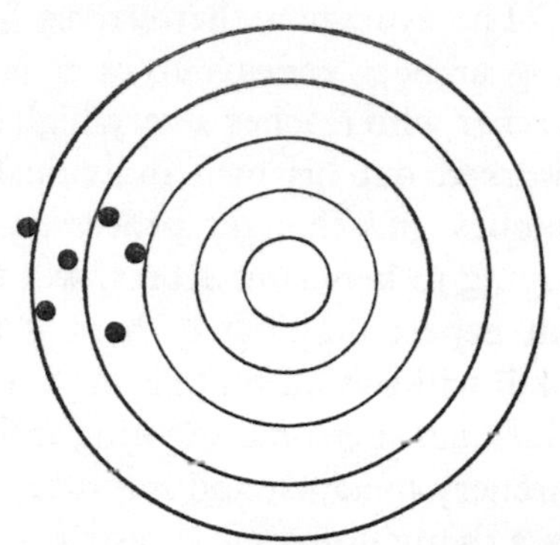

Fig. 37 Group of arrows to the left

face on release and another is to allow the string to hit the bracer or to foul loose clothing.

The mental approach

What makes a good archer? This is a question which has been answered many times and in many ways, but the accumulated wisdom of centuries can only instruct and prepare a novice for ultimate promotion to the ranks of those who find their pleasures in shooting in a bow. Mental concentration and precise co-ordination between mind and muscle are constant demands made on the archer and this fact becomes increasingly apparent to the beginner as he becomes more familiar with the art. As he progresses the application of the mind and its integration with his bodily actions assume greater importance.

Just what is demanded? How much should the archer give? How should it be given? Having studied theory, acquired the correct equipment and joined a club, what is now required of the novice to make everything work to turn him into a First Class Archer or even a Master Bowman? Alas, many will not become experts, few will find their way to the top and the greatest majority will shoot steadily on as average archers for years to come. All, however, will experience the same delightful pleasure in shooting.

The average archer strives for a better performance and the top archers endeavour to maintain their high standards. The archer who reaches a very high standard can be assumed to have worked out his own individual set of theories, shooting techniques and thought processes, and often the average shooter, trying to better his scores, will follow the paths trodden by such an expert desperately hoping that some of the championship skill will rub off on to him. Sometimes it does but more often it does not. Personal shooting techniques are the easiest aspects of archery to adjust and improve. What is more difficult to acquire is a thought process. Considerable volumes have been written on archery which deal variously with the subliminal process, and although recommendations in this respect are better avoided certain basic rules emerge which can be applied by any type of archer practising any form of archery.

Richard Carew writing in 1602[1] said that archery was a woman 'and her mind is passionate'; he could have added that she was also at times temperamental, sometimes incomprehensible and always a temptress with outstanding charms. On the same theme sayings of some of the oriental masters are suprisingly appropriate, 'The heart must be calm, because if it is occupied with anything other than archery, all effort put into shooting becomes void and in vain'—truly a demanding mistress. Acceptance of the inevitable mystery of femininity follows: 'No matter how much knowledge of archery a man may acquire and no matter how long he lives, he will not achieve complete mastery'—The exhilaration lies in the search!

A prescribed pattern of thought to suit a great number of individuals is not only problematical to prepare but extremely difficult to diffuse. What suits one will not suit another. And any such proposition for archery training would have to have perfection as its goal. Any scheme which could not fully justify itself by individual application should be rejected, which brings us back to reason that for every archer there is a separate and quite individual problem to be solved through his own endeavours. 'If he misses his mark, he should reflect on the reason for his

[1] Richard Carew: *The Survey of Cornwall* (1602).

failure and apply himself in earnest to eradicating the fault responsible for his miss, he should not become exasperated nor despair . . . nor should he revile himself or his bow or his arrows.' Sound advice of 600 years ago which still has a very practical application today.

Undoubtedly the mood of the archer has a great effect on his shooting, and as everyone is apt to feel 'up' at some times and 'down' at others some excuse for erratic performances can be made, but if it were possible to cultivate an 'archery mood' in preparation for shooting how much easier it would be to maintain a steady, albeit average, performance. To approach the shooting field with an anticipation of the pleasures to come, to take up the bow with confidence, and to commence to shoot with uninterrupted concentration are ideals hard to replace. It is extremely rare for a human being to be able to turn on a critical mental power; normally this is the result of a chain of thought, each individual devises his or her own sequence. To be able to give complete attention to a personal rhythm of shooting, without being distracted in any way, is a habit not too difficult to acquire and, once the habit has been learnt, easy to maintain. It clears the way for good shooting and ultimate personal satisfaction.

It is easy to be told not to do this or that and quite simple to correct faults if they are of a practical nature; it is also just as easy to be told to avoid a certain emotion but extremely difficult to quell a feeling of momentary anger, frustration or disappointment. Archery, in her many moods, can create these and other emotions which can break a smooth pattern of concentration and irreparably ruin a shot or even a day's shooting.

Roger Ascham, the celebrated academic toxophilite of the sixteenth century, echoing the sayings of many other masters, cautions us against giving way to anger and 'other affections' of the mind: 'It is when not only our bows, but our nerves are well strung, that we can do justice to the art.'

The search for 'the reason why' is important in the mental approach to archery, and the psychology of the sport includes a great amount of discussion with other archers which combines the dissemination of general archery know-how of a practical value with the elimination of individual doubts and queries. Some archers discover latent skills and others regain lost confidence after a mutual exchange of opinions and experiences and occasionally an opportunity of settling a problem left long unresolved presents itself at a week-end coaching school or a club archery quiz.

How fit does a person have to be before he or she can take up archery? A popular misconception is that great strength and stamina are necessary to draw powerful bows and that archery practice produces a muscle-bound torso and horny hands. It is not necessary to have great strength to draw modern bows, of which there is ample choice of suitable draw weights for ladies and gentlemen of all physiques, and the exertions from an afternoon of shooting are at least no more than those experienced after a country walk or a normal session of gardening. Drawing a bow produces similar physical benefits as would regular exercise designed to promote general well-being to the chest and shoulders, and a day of rhythmic but non-violent movement such as is produced by archery has long been recognized as beneficial to health.

6 · Etiquette and Safety

The 'unwritten rules' of archery is a contradiction in terms for these 'rules' have been written many times. They are rather guides to etiquette and to the observance of tradition, knowledge of which enables an archer not only to 'do the right thing' but to conform to the generally accepted procedures of the shooting field and tournament which, in the company of countless others, he has inherited. These are some of the things that help to make English archery rather special.

When six consecutive arrows are shot into the gold—known as a 'perfect end'—it was customary for everyone shooting the same round to pay one shilling (now 5p) to the archer responsible. This custom dates back more than 100 years and is normally recognized to apply to not less than 50 yards for ladies and 60 yards for gentlemen. If ladies and gentlemen are shooting the same round together and competing for the same prize then all pay the 'shillings'; if however they are shooting for separate prizes then the ladies are not expected to pay the 'shillings' to the men or vice versa. Although it is officially declared that 'there are no rules and never have been any about the payment of shillings for a perfect end' the Grand National Archery Society recognized this custom by formerly laying down the procedure for the collection of the shillings in their 'Duties of Judge and Field Captain' (1964).

Whilst shooting is in progress it is discourteous for any archer on the shooting line or elsewhere on the field to talk in a loud voice to the annoyance of others. It can be quite distracting to a person concentrating on shooting, particularly at the critical moment just before the 'loose', to be disturbed by a sudden noise of any kind and a thoughtless exclamation can, and often does, ruin what otherwise would have been a good shot.

Observers of human behaviour are unanimous in their assessment of a group of archers as being congenial and of one accord. But there are special moments when the individual, be he novice or champion, cogitates over some particular personal problem of shooting and at such moments resists the attempts of others to converse. It is then bad sportsmanship to talk to him if he obviously prefers to be silent.

The actual routine of shooting is under the control of an official if it is a tournament, or a member appointed to attend to such matters if it is a club shoot. Although the Judge or Field Captain, as such controllers of shooting are called, is responsible for the timing of shooting and the movement of archers to the targets he is unable to officiate over the unrestricted movements of archers when they are not actually shooting. Scores are normally recorded on sheets which are attached to boards for ease in handling, and in their competitive zest some archers stalk up and down the shooting line studying other archers' scores and comparing them with their own. The official controlling shooting has no power to prevent this, which is nevertheless considered very bad manners.

The third archer to shoot on a target is automatically appointed Target Captain. It is his duty to record all the scores of the archers shooting on his target and he relies on the co-operation of his 'butties' or target mates to make his task as trouble-free as possible. Not all archers look forward to this job but those who are fortunate enough to shoot without the additional responsibilities of this office can considerably assist the Target Captain by their compliance with the rules that apply—both written and unwritten. Often some shots fall behind the target, and when arrows are collected and scores taken it is bad form for an archer to go behind the target to retrieve those arrows 'in the green' before his scoring shots have been recorded. In recognition of the Target Captain's work throughout the shoot it is customary to thank him at the end of a round, and it has become almost a tradition for all the archers present to give three cheers for the Field Captain at the end of a day's shooting.

Some archers pay considerable sums of money for their equipment, others prefer to make their own or to provide for themselves very economically, but whatever the value, these possessions are highly prized by their owners and a good archer cares for his equipment like a mother for her child. Indiscriminate handling of bows and arrows by others is looked upon with the utmost disfavour and, unless permission to do so is sought and given, it is extremely bad manners to touch another's equipment.

Accidents can happen, and when an archer breaks another's arrow through his own carelessness, he pays for it on the spot.

Some shoot quickly, others take more time, and it may happen that an archer who shoots more slowly than others or who, for some reason, has not been able to keep up with his fellow shooters, is still standing when others have finished. It is bad manners to leave him alone still shooting on the line, and his neighbour should remain patiently until all arrows have been discharged. When going to or from the shooting line an archer should always 'keep to the left' to avoid colliding with others. This rule of the road is simply observed and can save the confusion and indignity of being locked in a momentary embrace with an opponent—bow, arrows and all.

The G.N.A.S. *Rules of Shooting* contain several polite reminders of tradition, pointing out what is expected of archers in certain situations, rather than forcefully declaring that such matters are inflexible rules. For example, 'Any archer who has won one or more of the Society's medals is expected to wear one at least at every subsequent Championship or Handicap Meeting at which he or she shall compete.' And included in the Dress Regulations . . . 'The accepted dress should be encouraged whenever organized shooting takes place including Club Target Days.'

Safety precautions

Serious consideration must be given to the lethal nature of bows and arrows and, in common with any sporting activity which could have fatal results if not properly managed, certain safety rules must be rigidly observed. Generally speaking these rules are contained in the G.N.A.S. *Rules of Shooting* for Target Archery and despite the inevitability of repetition further comment is offered on some of the most important points.

Fortunately, as far as accidents to life and limb are concerned, archery in this country can boast an unblemished record, although the authorities have been aware of the possibility of a bystander being hit by a flying arrow since Tudor times at least. It was during the reign of Henry VIII that a law was made absolving archers from any responsibility if they accidentally injured or killed a passerby, provided they were shooting at recognized butts and so long as they cried 'Fast' as a warning that shooting was in progress. These two essential safety factors which applied 500 years ago obtain today.

Firstly, shooting should take place at an archery field officially recognized as such. The indiscriminate use of gardens, parks, common land or public places, no matter how safe they may appear, is contrary to the current official rules, and any archery practice which takes place under such arrangements would not be recognized, either for insurance purposes or in connexion with the recording of scores under the various schemes approved by G.N.A.S.

The shooting ground itself should be adequately surveyed for possible danger areas and appropriate steps should be taken to make it quite safe. A sparse hedge next to a busy public thoroughfare is insufficient protection, for instance, against sudden incursions of small boys, curious about the activity but innocent of the danger lurking in the sudden flash of a badly loosed arrow. Numerous other situations can be envisaged where a little thought, coupled with some slight rearrangement of the direction of shooting or the erection of a simple protective barrier, could possibly save many anxious moments.

Secondly, the use of the word 'Fast'. It has been demonstrated that, as an archers' warning, it can claim considerable antiquity and as such it is still used today. Its origin may date from the days when the commander of some medieval battalion of archers, directing barrage after barrage of arrows, stopped the shooting by the cry of 'Stand Fast' whilst redeployment took place, or whilst new tactics were being devised and, once the bowmen had taken up their new positions or the enemy came within bowshot, the command 'Loose' sent yet another massed flight of shafts into the air. Whatever the origins, the expression 'Fast' has a firmly established usage of such potency that whenever this urgent cry rings out on the archery field shooting ceases immediately and without question.

Some archers take unnecessary risks which can, at best, be disconcerting to others and in turn this can lead to bad shooting, the archer's attention having been distracted and worried by potential dangers. Thus it is logical to assume that by the elimination of practices which are dangerous the way is cleared for uninterrupted concentration on good shooting and it is only by understanding the rules of safety that misfortune can be avoided. To eliminate the danger of an accidentally released shaft, archers soon get into the habit of aiming a drawn arrow only in the direction of the target—and in fact this is a Rule of Shooting which must be enforced by club and tournament officials.

Each archer must have complete mastery over every shot, and to aim indiscriminately without knowing where the arrow will land is thoughtless and an unforgivable practice. The unpredictability of an arrow shot straight into the air or the danger of a shaft shot so that it goes out of sight, over an obstacle or into bushes for instance, illustrates the type of uncontrolled shooting to be avoided. In any case there is very little satisfaction in undisciplined archery as, after all, the whole idea is to hit the target, whether it be a conventional 4 ft. boss or an animal face on a field course, and so perhaps a useful text, hung prominently on the club notice board, could well read—'Think before you shoot.'

It is also important to exercise complete control over the movement of everyone on the archery field, no matter whether they are taking part in the shooting, or are there as spectators or visitors, and the rules are quite clear on this point. All those shooting should move to the targets together on a signal given by whoever is in charge of the shooting. The reason for this is obvious; unordered arrangements in the matter of moving to or from the targets could lead to persons still being in the danger area, to their peril, when others are waiting to shoot. Five yards to the rear of the actual shooting line there should exist a demarcation line, often marked but sometimes imaginary, which divides the shooting field from the resting area. No archer is allowed in front of this line unless he is engaged in shooting or walking to and from the shooting line. This gap then is a neutral area kept uncluttered by tackle and benches—a protective barrier preventing overcrowding on the shooting line and helping to reduce distractions caused by the close proximity of those not shooting. Well behind this five-yard line is the waiting area, and fifteen yards further back are the spectators, without, it is hoped, too many transistorized distractions.

Much has been written on the recognized methods of keeping equipment in good order. Apart from the deterioration of efficiency resulting from badly maintained tackle and the actual loss of valuable items through breakage due to lack of attention, another risk which has to be taken by those who do not look after their equipment is that of personal injury. A frayed string can give way and the result can be a broken bow plus a black eye, a splinter can lift on a wooden arrow and if the shaft is not immediately rejected a gashed bow hand can be the reward, or maybe a bruised forearm can be experienced through the absence of a suitable bracer. Although such minor injuries would not be serious in themselves they are by no means honourable wounds—in fact the display of such scars would only publicly proclaim the inefficiency of the archer and the inadequacy of those that taught him.

The best way to draw an arrow from a target is to pull it out gently in exactly the opposite direction from which it entered, grasping it as near as possible to the target with one hand, with the other held flat on the target face close to the arrow. This prevents the arrow from being bent on withdrawal which could easily happen if it were pulled out roughly at an angle, and also protects the target face from being damaged by torn or enlarged arrow holes (see Fig. 38). Those arrows which penetrate a target,

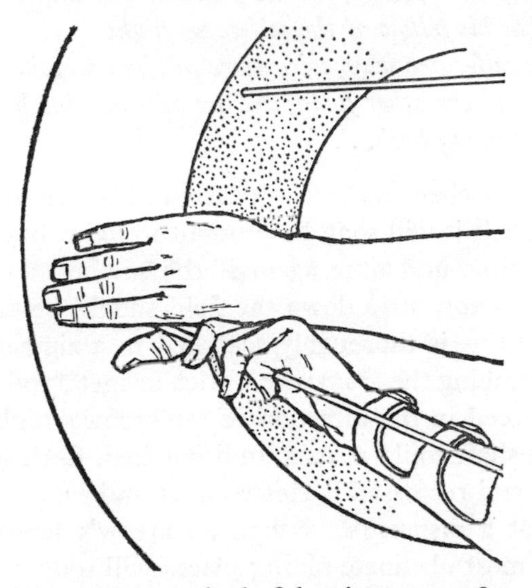

Fig. 38 The correct method of drawing arrows from a target

often near the edge, right up to and including some of the fletchings should be withdrawn from the back of the boss. This is to prevent the fletchings from being ripped off.

Occasionally an arrow which misses the target completely, in utter disgust at its own performance, hides itself in shame flat in the grass. When it is located—be careful not to tread on it—it should be retrieved by pulling it through the grass in line with its flight. This again preserves the fletching, and prevents undue bending which could occur through clumsy recovery.

Sometimes an arrow, having missed the target, will defy discovery and remain hidden, much to the annoyance of its owner and the impatience of others waiting to shoot. The annoyance and impatience are soon dissipated when the cry goes up 'Got it!'—but just how should one go about 'getting it'? How can an arrow, completely concealed under neatly cropped grass, be found quickly? There are no short cuts despite the often quoted recommendation in Shakespeare's *Merchant of Venice*. He makes Bassanio say:

> *'In my school days, when I had lost one shaft,*
> *I shot his fellow of the self-same flight*
> *The self-same way, with more advised watch,*
> *To find the other forth, and by adventuring both,*
> *I oft found both. . . .'*

If several archers make a concerted effort to search for the offending shaft it will soon be brought to light, but it can easily be missed time and time again if the method adopted is not orderly. A narrow strip down the field should be taken by each archer, and this is thoroughly searched in a zig-zag fashion by carefully combing the grass with a stick or metal rod. It is important to proceed in the direction of the arrow's flight, otherwise the hidden shaft could remain undiscovered. Each sector should be crossed and recrossed in this manner and each line should be advanced at a distance less than an arrow's length. By these means the most obstinate hiding places will soon be revealed.

Use the tassel to wipe each arrow as it is retrieved, particularly if it has been in the ground, and inspect it to see that the fletchings are intact, make sure it has not been bent or dented and see that pile and nock are as they should be.

7 · The Club

How does an archery club fit into existing organization of archery as a sport in this country, and what advantages are there in being a member of such a club? This is a question frequently asked by those who have an active interest in the sport but do not belong to any club or society which exists for this sport alone or combines it with several other activities. There are those clubs, for instance, which have several sections, each practising a different sport, but sharing a ground and amenities. This arrangement is often to be found in a works club, and archers finding themselves members of firms offering such facilities are fortunate in having excellent opportunities for pursuing their interest. Usually such clubs are closed to all but employees of the organization concerned. The majority of clubs catering exclusively for archery are open to everyone and are individually organized and administered. There are special societies which exist to cater for disabled persons, schools, police cadets, the services and so on.

Affiliation

Apart from the competitive and social aspects there are other special advantages in belonging to a club; for example it is far more economical to purchase equipment for a group activity rather than for individual use. The less obvious advantages are vested in what is known as affiliation to the parent body. Once a club is formed and has a set of constitutional rules and is being run by a committee elected by its members, it can apply to the Grand National Archery Society for affiliation status. The

G.N.A.S., which has been the governing body for archery in the United Kingdom since 1950, administers through regional societies, and imposes an annual levy for each member of a club which becomes affiliated. This confers certain benefits to the clubs generally and to individual members in particular. The whole organization and activities of the G.N.A.S. are co-ordinated by a central council, the honorary officers of which are elected by the general body of members and in addition each regional society sends representatives who take an active part in the Society's affairs.

The G.N.A.S. is a Member Association of the Fédération Internationale de Tir à l'Arc (F.I.T.A.), which was formed in

Fig. 39 The badge of the Grand National Archery Society

1931, and this body is responsible amongst other things for the promotion of World Championships which are held biennially. The Member Associations of F.I.T.A. range from the numerical superiority of the National Archery Association of the United States to archery associations of lesser countries whose enthusiasm compensates for their small memberships.

Each club in this country which is affiliated to G.N.A.S. through a regional society has the advantage of automatically participating in a group insurance scheme without extra payment. The cover given is in respect of damage or injury caused in the course of the sport, in any form anywhere in the United Kingdom, but only when the shooting is under the auspices of the G.N.A.S. or an affiliated body. The indemnity is on account of legal liability only and does not insure an individual in respect of personal injuries such as are covered by Personal Accident insurance policies. The operative clause is 'under the auspices of the G.N.A.S. or an affiliated body' and, therefore, any practice not organized by a club or any meeting or demonstration not officially recognized cannot be covered by this scheme.

Attracting members

Although this chapter contains much that is primarily intended for the organizers of a club, a great deal of the information that follows is of general interest to the ordinary member. It is undoubtedly true that the most important member of a club is its newest recruit. To exist at all a club must not only have a healthy membership but this must be maintained by regular new arrivals. Archery in this country has a very high annual wastage rate—possibly a fifth of the general membership leaves the sport each year—it is quite obvious therefore that to keep an economic level of membership an intake in the order of one fifth must be sought after. This then is clear proof that, in addition to attracting new members to a club, the interest of the shooting members must be nurtured so that they remain. Many archers take up the sport enthusiastically enough to begin with, but because of a lukewarm attitude in the club to a planned campaign to keep those members they soon drift off to take up some other sport or hobby. Many of the aspects which can attract new members and at the same time help to keep old ones are worthy of careful study. Let us consider some of them.

Regular publicity is of untold value: but publicity of archery purely as a sport is a difficult matter and can present quite a problem. Although it has been said that any form of publicity is good, this does not necessarily apply to archery. It will readily be seen that undisciplined individuals involving themselves in Robin Hood antics, aimlessly shooting small game or even domestic animals, or equally immature show-offs re-enacting childish escapades which have even extended to live William Tell stunts, can do great harm to the public image of archery in this country. Many such items find their way into the pages of the local paper and present to its readers a wrong impression of archery as it is really practised. What then is good publicity as far as archery is concerned? How can the local paper—usually most co-operative—be used to the best advantage to attract potential members and to enhance the sport in the eyes of the public? A most effective and simple idea is a more or less permanent notice to the effect that 'The Blankers Archery Club meet at the Sports Field on anyday at X o'clock' followed, of course, by the name and address of secretary or chairman. Some towns publish a 'What's On' diary in which this notice could appear, or a useful display medium is the public library notice board or a local sports shop.

Correct archery terminology should be employed in any written account of meetings and a little extra time explaining these terms to an enthusiastic but uninitiated reporter will pay dividends. Simple examples of what should be avoided include: hitting the 'bullseye' instead of the 'gold,' 'firing' the bow instead of 'shooting' it, 'playing bows and arrows' instead of the time honoured expression 'shooting in a bow' and so on. If a photograph can be included so much the better, but do please ensure that those photographed are neatly and correctly dressed and that attention to background is given to convey the best possible impression to the public. Avoid the gimmicky pose and the stunt picture no matter how hard the photographer 'with a new angle' tries. The average club archer can be excused a faulty style but never a sloppy presentation for publicity purposes. A successful press picture will encourage the photographer to return. National publicity is unnecessary except for national events and the 'local rag' is by far the best medium for the local club.

Demonstrations

Perhaps an opportunity to stage a demonstration will present itself at a fête or exhibition of some kind and this form of publicity, handled correctly, can be invaluable. The most important aspect of such demonstrations is that they provide an opportunity of making personal contact with the public. The actual demonstration itself can be quite simple and *should be kept short.* Archery is not a spectator sport, and those who find themselves attracted will be more interested in talking about it to an archer for ten minutes than seeing thirty minutes of shooting. Make sure the audience know what is happening, nothing is more infuriating than to stand and watch archers, shooting apparently aimlessly at targets. What are they aiming to hit? How do they score? Who goes first? Are all the bows the same? What are the arrows made of?—A series of simple questions will immediately crowd into the enquiring mind and those taking part must be prepared for these and other questions which must be answered simply and clearly. Try to keep the archers and the targets well within view of the audience, do not employ too many stunts and above all have smart and properly dressed participants. Discuss with the organizers the detailed arrangements and safety precautions and stick to a rigid time-table. Lastly ensure that the function is recognized as an official fixture of the club by recording in the minutes the formal approval of the committee or general meeting beforehand. The last point has a very practical application. If an archery event is organized by a club which is affiliated to the Grand National Archery Society, that function is automatically covered by the group insurance scheme which would apply to normal club target days, provided, of course, that care had been taken to run the event on a basis which satisfied all the applicable G.N.A.S. Rules.

Enthusiastic participation in local activities fulfils the third clause of the *Constitution* of the Grand National Archery Society, which reads: 'The objects of the Society shall be the promotion and encouragement of Archery in all its forms...' and many and diverse are the functions in which a local club might be called to take part; fêtes and carnivals, lectures and demonstrations, invitations to participate in festivals, special displays and even as consultants for theatrical presentations, are only some of the many ways in which the specialized knowledge of the graceful art of archery can be disseminated. Thus a new member not only has a new and exciting sport revealed to him but can immediately feel part of an organization which has some local standing and is recognized as a live amenity of the district.

Let us assume that we have attracted a potential new member, how is he (or she) to be dealt with ? The first impression is always a lasting one and the newcomer must be put at his ease and gradually and informally introduced to other members. There should be no lack of assistance as far as basic instruction is concerned and archers are invariably willing to be helpful to new members. If the club boasts a member who is qualified as an Instructor the new arrival is very fortunate, but at worst an experienced old hand will take over and put the prospective archer through the early stages of instruction. Brief details should be given regarding essential information such as 'what it costs' and 'when the club meets' plus other minor administrative matters, even the arrangements for tea. The rules which apply on the field will be imparted as instruction progresses and a copy of the club general rules should be handed over as soon as possible. The fixture list should be explained and 101 questions answered. The important thing is, that a new member must feel an integral part of the club as soon as possible and not just the newest member.

A great amount of advice has been given on how to maintain the first enthusiasm and keep the interest of the members. The primary aim should be to ensure a happy club with activities to appeal to all ages and both sexes. There should be a programme of varied activities throughout the season which should emphasize events on the home ground. In addition to Target Archery, Clout, Rovers, Field Shooting wherever possible and some novelty rounds can be included. Facilities must be given for the top-class shots to get practice under competitive conditions as well as special arrangements needed for beginners. Social activity, especially in the winter, is invaluable in helping to hold the 'family' together and again these features must be included in the list of club fixtures. A dinner combined with the annual prize-giving, a Christmas party, talks and discussion evenings, film shows—these are only some of the social events which can be included. A very popular feature would be the inclusion of one or two practical sessions dealing with such matters as string making, fletching or tackle maintenance.

Mention has been made earlier of officially published material of common value and importance to archers; whereas a certain section of the archery community are easily able to absorb the more detailed aspects of such publications, others perfunctorily dismiss them as being too labyrinthine.

Many archers find difficulty in fully understanding the Handicap and Classification Schemes which, at first sight, do seem somewhat complex, and they are quite content to leave everything to the club official whose task it is to keep scores records. Although optional the great majority of clubs take advantage of these official schemes which are operated quite independently of each other, all the administration being conducted on a club level.

So that the ability of individual archers can be assessed the Handicap Scheme is used, and in order that their achievements can be recognized by awards of titles according to the shooting standards reached, the Classification Scheme is operated. These schemes are occasionally reviewed to bring them into line with the current demands of higher scores and they have a wide appeal in club archery.

A club Records Officer is appointed who has the interesting but exacting task of keeping a record of each member's scores and their subsequent gradings under both of these schemes. From these records progress can be observed, success can be rewarded and accurate allowances made for use in tournaments when prizes are awarded on a handicap basis.

The Classification Scheme

In the Classification Scheme certain titles are awarded to archers according to their level of performance. The qualifications required become progressively more difficult until the exalted rank of 'Grand Master Bowman' is reached, but although few archers reach this exacting standard there is ample scope in the lesser ranks of 'Master Bowman', and Class I, II and III Archers. This scheme is operated quite simply: to gain Class I, II or III an archer must shoot, during the calendar year, three rounds of, or better than, the scores set out below. These rounds must be shot at a Club Target Day[1] and under G.N.A.S. Rules of Shooting or at a meeting organized by G.N.A.S. or a body affiliated to it. Immediately the requisite scores are made the upgrading occurs, but if during a second year the archer is unable to make the necessary scores in his class then he is automatically relegated to the class below on 1st January of the third year.

QUALIFYING SCORES

Class I, II and III Archers

Gentlemen	*York*	*F.I.T.A.*	*St. George*	*New Western*	*New National*	*Long Metric*	*Short Metric*	*Hereford*	*Albion*	*Long Western*	*Long National*	*Western*	*National*	*Windsor*	*American*
1st Class	800	980	644	515	370	434									
2nd Class	620	820	516	391	276	339	481	806	642	526	378				
3rd Class	450	650	388	275	191	245	404	633	517	410	289	521	382	629	524

Ladies	*Hereford*	*F.I.T.A.*	*Albion*	*Long Western*	*Long National*	*Long Metric*	*Short Metric*	*Western*	*National*	*Windsor*	*American*
1st Class	800	895	639	522	374	421					
2nd Class	620	710	511	400	279	324	384	523	382	635	529
3rd Class	450	530	383	286	195	232	297	406	294	510	425

The supreme titles of Grand Master Bowman and Master Bowman are treated specially: the standard of the former has been made very high indeed and qualification can only be gained at major tournaments, whereas, although the standard of Master

[1] A Club Target Day is any day and time appointed under the rules of the club for shooting a pre-determined round, all scores made being recorded in the club's Score Book, as opposed to any other day when the club permits its members to use the ground for practice and when scores are not recorded.

Bowman is high, it is frequently secured on what amounts to a club level. It will be seen from the qualifications required that the internationally used F.I.T.A. Round is included and that attendance at a major meeting is essential. This is because archers shooting to such standards become eligible for selection to take part in World Championship meetings. Coveted badges, which can be worn in perpetuity, are presented to holders of Grand Master Bowman and Master Bowman classifications.

QUALIFYING ROUNDS AND SCORES

Grand Master Bowman

Ladies	*Gentlemen*
3 F.I.T.A. Rounds of at least 1,200	3 F.I.T.A. Rounds of at least 1,220

All rounds must be shot in one calendar year at meetings organized by F.I.T.A., G.N.A.S. or a Regional Society.

Master Bowman

Ladies	*Gentlemen*
3 Hereford Rounds of at least 1,000	3 York Rounds of at least 1,000
1 F.I.T.A. Rounds of at least 1,100	1 F.I.T.A. Rounds of at least 1,150

All rounds must be shot in one calendar year. Two may be shot at a club tournament or target day and two must be shot at a meeting organized by F.I.T.A., G.N.A.S., Regional Society or County Association.

The Handicap Scheme

The Handicap Scheme is also administered by individual clubs and a set of Handicap Tables is issued by the G.N.A.S. which includes precise instructions for operating the scheme. The principle by which this scheme works is that the score of any given round has a corresponding handicap figure, based on the presumption that a score of 800 for a York Round equals 0 or scratch. Scratch scores for each of twelve rounds have been assessed and handicap figures ranging from 60 to —40 are matched by their corresponding scores. Thus any archer whether he be average or expert, shooting a standard round, can easily find the handicap equivalent for his score. This figure is reduced as the archer's performance improves according to a straightforward set of rules which are easily assimilated and simple to apply.

A Handicap Figure provides the individual archer with a ready means of making comparisons of his scores over a season which would otherwise be well-nigh impossible. Additional to this yardstick by which personal progress can be measured are useful tables, included in the official handicap publication, showing the score anticipated for each dozen arrows shot at different distances according to a specified handicap figure. With a handicap figure available an allowance can be allocated to an archer so that he can compete on an equal basis against archers of a higher or lower standard; it will be apparent that the lower the standard of the archer the greater will be his handicap allowance. Different sets of tables are used for Ladies and Gentlemen, and Juniors.

The cost of archery

Enquiries from prospective archers always include questions as to the expenditure necessary for equipment and the sort of subscriptions they are likely to be asked to pay. Despite the fact that this is an important publicity factor for the sport, it is a subject quite often inaccurately quoted and, possibly due to the reluctance of the Englishman to discuss intimate matters of finance, insufficiently explained.

Early advice on the purchase of equipment is very necessary. Equipment made to extremely high standards and of superior quality can be purchased at reasonable prices, and it is up to the individual to decide what he can afford for his chosen sport. No matter whether his choice is a bow costing £5 or one costing as much as £150 his appreciation of archery cannot be measured in proportion to expenditure. Costly equipment does not automatically produce first-class shots but, as any lady who treats herself to a new hat will confirm, the acquisition of a new model—bow or hat—gives the new owner a psychological advantage over others and can be a powerful boost to morale.

Club subscriptions generally are low, in comparison with some other sports, but these will naturally vary from town to town and according to facilities and amenities offered. Usually no extra subscriptions are payable except in the case of specially organized meetings and tournaments when separate target fees are required. Compared with other forms of amusement and sporting activities archery can be said to be most reasonable and well within anyone's purse.

Traditions of archery

Reference has been made to the ancient traditions of archery—traditions which reflect the love of a very special kind of group pursuit, where a number of like-minded persons have organized themselves into a society or club devoted to toxophily. It has been said that whenever Englishmen meet the first thing they do is to form a club, and it is because of this tendency that records of group activities have been handed down. These now form the traditions of the past to be enjoyed and jealously protected today. It is a comforting thought that perhaps in this modern age we are also making traditions so that future generations can look back with, perhaps, nostalgia, envy, or even amusement. If our activities are worth enjoying the memories of them are worth preserving.

How can this be done by an archery club, whose officials are really no more than ordinary members devoting a little more of their leisure time to attend to all the many extra jobs required to make the club run smoothly? Isn't there enough to do without recording what may seem insignificant events just for our grandchildren to wonder at and giggle over?

Every club is important, no matter how small, and in every group of people enjoying archery the pattern of the season's shooting unfolds, special occasions are celebrated, records are made, perfect ends are shot, new archers are born, and customs become established. To conform to the regulations of the governing body of archery each club has to be 'properly constituted' and, briefly, this involves having a democratically elected committee and a set of constitutional rules. The Constitution of a club is the legal base on which it stands and contains instructions as to how the club shall be governed. The club may find it necessary to amplify the G.N.A.S. *Rules of Shooting* so as to include local restrictions governing activities on the shooting ground. The Minute Book of the club's committee and general meetings, at which notice can be taken of any special events, will automatically form the record aimed at for posterity. The names of prizewinners should be noted in the club's Score Book.

Modern clubs are recommended to consider many of the principles exemplified by some of the older and more experienced clubs. Fashions change and individuals vary their pattern of likes and dislikes over the years and although many small, but important, aspects of archery remain constant the compilers of rules and regulations must move with the times, giving consideration to the up-to-date demands of the contemporary archer. At the same time they must maintain a traditional pattern of the sport which, despite the revolutionary advances it has experienced in recent years, remains very much part of Old England.

Archery club rules

To assist newly formed clubs in framing their rules and as a guide to older clubs who plan a revision of those already in use a selection of the most important items which should be incorporated is given below.

It is advisable to produce a set of rules couched in simple terms, rather than in quasi-legal phraseology, which are essentially workable and which allow for all contingencies. Aim to be brief and concise.

Every member of a club is bound by the current club rules and therefore he or she is entitled to a copy of them.

1. The name of the Club shall be the Blanksville Bowmen.

2. The object of the Club shall be the practice and promotion of Archery.

3. The Club shall consist of a President, Chairman, Hon.

Secretary, Hon. Treasurer, Shooting Members and Non-shooting Associates.

4. The management of the Club shall be entrusted to a Committee elected annually.

5. The Committee shall consist of a Chairman, Hon. Secretary, Hon. Treasurer, and . . . members (from 3–6 according to total membership). (*a*)

6. There shall be a General Meeting held once a year to elect Officers and Committee, and to make or alter rules, etc. (*b*)

7. A quorum shall consist of fifty per cent of the total membership.

8. The accounts of the Club shall be submitted to the General Meeting once a year.

9. Every Shooting Member shall pay an annual subscription of £. . . . ., Juniors (under 18) shall pay £. . . . and Non-shooting Associates £. . . . . (*c*)

10. Subscriptions become due on (1st April) each year.

11. The election of new members shall be finally decided by the Committee. Names of candidates for membership should be exhibited, together with the names of their Proposers and Seconders, and if no objection is registered, the Committee will elect.

12. Visitors shall be allowed to shoot at any Practice or Prize Meetings, being introduced by a member (either free or by payment of small fee). (*d*)

13. Any member whose subscription is (one year) in arrears shall be liable to have his/her name removed from the list of members and not re-elected or entitled to shoot at any of the Club Meetings until all such arrears are paid.

14. Non-shooting Associates shall have no part in the management of the Club.

15. The *Rules of Shooting* of the Grand National Archery Society shall be observed.

16. The Shooting Season will commence on . . . and terminate on. . . . . (*e*)

17. A Practice Meeting will be held on . . . . each week during the season.

18. Two Prize Meetings will be held each year, the dates to be fixed by the Committee. (*f*)

19. Monthly Handicap Meetings shall be held.

20. A team of not less than six members of another club shall be challenged each year to compete with a similar number of members of this Club.

21. Anyone presenting a Prize to the Club shall have the right to regulate the terms on which it shall be awarded, subject to the approval of the Committee.

22. No archer shall be awarded more than one Club Prize at any meeting.

23. The Secretary for the time being has charge of, and legal possession of, all the property of the Club.

24. Any matters not covered by the foregoing Rules will be dealt with at the discretion of the Committee.

Notes

(*a*) *If the activities of the Club merit it additional Officers can be elected such asField Captain, Social Member, etc.*

(*b*) *The procedure for issuing notices for General and other Meetings must be agreed and rigidly adhered to. Usually 10 to 14 days' notice will be ample.*

(*c*) *Arrangements can be made to include a 'family' subscription. If members join late in the season a* pro-rata *reduction is often made for the initial subscription.*

(*d*) *Some clubs arrange for visitors to shoot, say, three times before they need to decide to join or not. In this case subscriptions can be reduced by any visitor's fees paid.*

(*e*) *The date, time, and round selected for all Club Target Days should be published beforehand so that any scores submitted for record and classification purposes can be officially recognized.*

(*f*) *It is advisable to provide a standard form of score sheet for the use of club members. A specimen layout, which permits scoring of any standard round, is given on the following page* (See Fig. 40.)

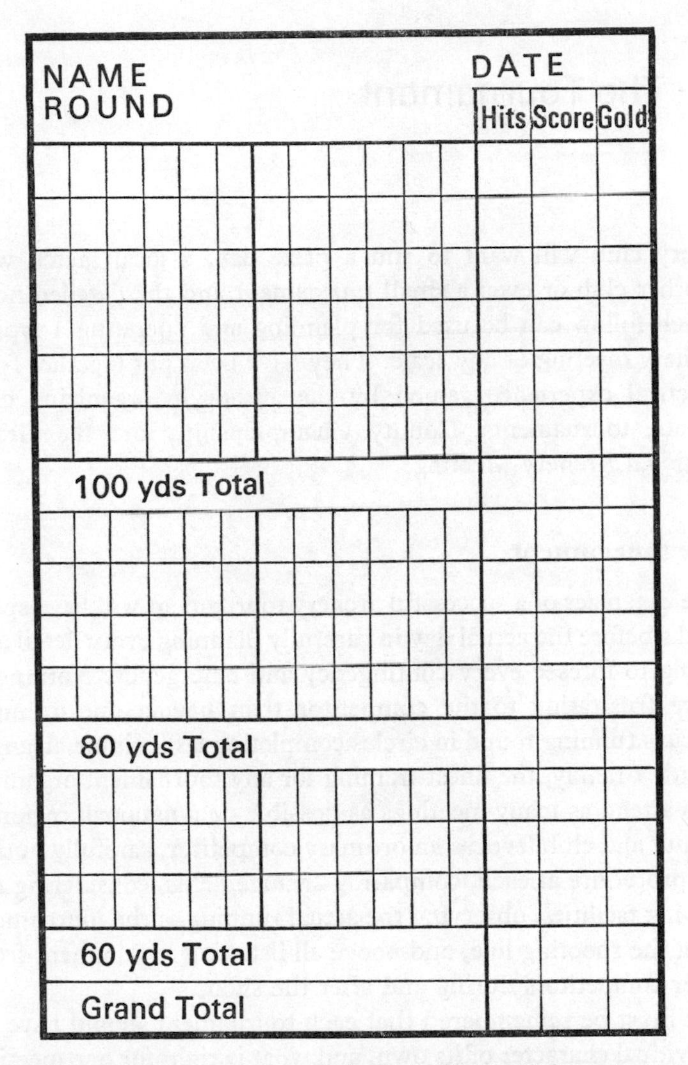

Fig. 40 Specimen score sheet which can be used for any standard round

8 · The Tournament

Every club will want to run a prize day, a local match with another club or even a small tournament and the detailed notes which follow can be used for planning and operating a typical archery meeting of any scale. They have been put together from practical experience gained by the author in organizing club events, tournaments, County Championships and the Grand National Archery Meeting.

The tournament

The organizer of a successful archery tournament will have spent weeks before the actual day in carefully planning every detail and trying to foresee every contingency and emergency. Nothing is more frustrating to the competitor than having one or more officials running round in circles completing last-minute arrangements. Frankly, the finest training for any tournament organizer is to attend as many meetings as possible on a national, regional, county and club level as an ordinary competitor, carefully noting the procedure at each, comparing arrangements, considering the varying facilities, observing the actual running of the tournament from the shooting line, and above all listening to comment from other competitors during and after the shoot.

It must be remembered that each tournament should have an individual character of its own, and what is right for one meeting need not necessarily be so for another. An example of this is the use of large numbers pinned to the backs of competitors at international competitions: an important and useful feature for these particular meetings, but archers shooting precisely the same round at a club shoot would be completely out of place with such insignia and there would be absolutely no need for such identification. This, of course, is an extreme example, but unnecessary labour, time and trouble can be avoided by carefully balancing the features of a tournament to suit its character and individuality.

There are several phases of a tournament which can be discussed in turn and it is emphasized that attention to precise detail will help considerably to make the meeting a success from both the competitive and social aspect, whether it be your own club prize day or a full-scale meeting of national importance. The complete organization of a tournament can be grouped under four main headings each of which includes a number of specific tasks, the smooth integration of which combines to cover every aspect of running a tournament. The four headings, with individual sub-division of tasks, are as follows:

1. *Planning*
   The Tournament Organizer and committee
   Choice of ground and date
   Rounds and awards
   Appointment of officials
   Recruiting helpers
   Supply of equipment
   Catering and extra features

2. *Publicity*
   Publicity and timing
   The entry form and prospectus
   Local newspapers
   Target lists

3. *Field Arrangements*
   General layout of field
   Timing
   Scoring

4. *Post-Tournament Procedure*
   Prizegiving
   Clearing the field
   Publishing results
   Settling the account

1. Planning

The over-all organization must be in the hands of a specified committee or one individual. Often a club committee will decide on general policy and delegate the actual running of the tournament to one of its officers. It is little use asking one person to run a shoot without precise and exact directions from the governing body as to how that shoot should be run. Valuable guiding principles are laid down in the Regulations for the National Championship Meeting and of course any tournament run by a club or society affiliated to the Grand National Archery Society must adhere to the official *Rules of Shooting* published by that body.

Choice of ground

Availability will naturally be the main factor in the choice of a suitable ground for an archery meeting, and ideally it should be flat with well mown grass, a neutral background of trees if possible, ample width to accommodate the expected number of targets (plus a reasonable margin) and long enough to allow for a space beyond the targets of at least 40 yards of smooth turf, or 15 yards of turf backed by a steep grass bank at least 8 ft. high and a similar distance behind the shooting line. For an all-day shoot the ground should be such that the shooting line faces north-east, or so arranged that the maximum sunlight falls on the target faces during shooting. Space for visitors must be clearly marked and the important details of ladies' and gentlemen's toilets, car parking facilities and catering accommodation must be borne in mind.

Local regulations must be investigated and if necessary complied with, such as the avoidance of a cricket 'table', siting the targets so that public access, if allowed, is not barred and due consideration given to any other local aspects affecting layout and safety.

The date must be chosen well in advance after carefully consulting the calendar of archery events, and it is advisable to allow for the peak holiday period.

Rounds and awards

The choice of rounds will be governed by several factors and their selection must depend on the type of function being planned and the type of archer the meeting is going to attract; for instance it could be a friendly shoot or a fiercely competitive tournament. Another consideration is the time factor. The recognized 'prize' rounds, York, Hereford and F.I.T.A., are shot at national, regional and county championships and with an all-day shoot these major rounds can be completed comfortably, but if only half a day is envisaged a shorter round would be more popular.

An important, and sometimes controversial, aspect is the prize list. Usually prizes are awarded to the first three places (or more if the entry permits) the best gold[1] of each round shot, the greatest number of golds, possibly the best score at each of the distances and in recent years the awarding of a separate series of awards on a handicap basis. Quite often the Lady Paramount will want to present her own personal prizes and in this case she will invariably specify the conditions of their award. Occasionally the matter of awarding these prizes will be left to the organizer and in this case they are customarily presented for the 'next unrewarded score' for lady and gentleman.

For an established meeting a collection of Challenge Trophies will grace the prize table but expending a lot of money from tournament profits on such articles, which to be good are usually

[1] 'Best Golds' can be measured by using a specially shaped card. This is placed flat on the target with the notch against the arrow and the position of the pinhole marked on the card together with the archer's name (see Fig. 41).

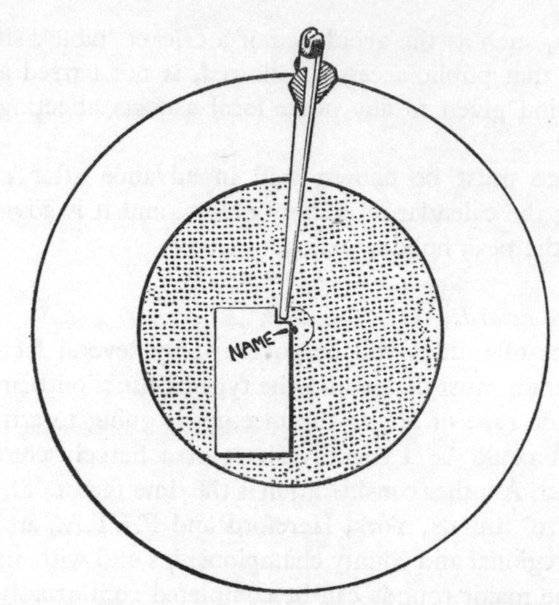

Fig. 41 The use of a measuring card to determine a 'best gold'

quite expensive, in the early years of a tournament, is to be avoided. Many such trophies have tarnished, and gathered dust in a secondhand dealer's window after a brief and glorious life in service with a once or twice only meeting. Far better to wait until the tournament has established itself as a regular event before considering such embellishments. Occasionally, on the other hand, benefactors who have the interests of the sport at heart or a very suitable trophy in the attic, have come forward and made a presentation. The conditions governing the awarding of such gifts should be subject to the approval of the organizing body. Special interest can be cultivated by the award of a trophy of curious or local interest or of special antiquarian value such as an ancient arrowhead suitably mounted or a hunting horn appropriately inscribed.

A selection of medals which can bear the date, the name of the meeting (often abbreviated) and class of award are almost standard prizes at an archery meeting, and these can be supplied by one of the stockists of archery equipment who carry a wide range of tasteful designs for this purpose. The awarding of prizes for novelty aspects is not always acceptable at a meeting which is primarily competitive; however, there is a time and place for everything and often a lighthearted touch can be an advantage at a local friendly tournament. The element of chance should be strictly reserved for the novelty shoot, apart from an award which is always accepted with good humour, and in fact has been a tradition of archery for many years. It is the presentation of a wooden spoon—usually for the worst 'white' at the last end.

Entry fees should be carefully assessed so that the individual archer's expenses are not too excessive, but at the same time it must be remembered that the overheads of the tournament must be met. The initial guesswork can only be proved an accurate assessment after the final accounting. It is not good policy to make too high a profit, although a small surplus carried over to the following year can be a great advantage.

Appointment of officials

Early in the planning stages of a tournament the services of various officials should be secured, and it cannot be emphasized too strongly that at least one of these should be an archer of wide experience, with tact and a thorough knowledge of the rules and procedure applicable. Archery meetings of the past were graced with a lady patroness who generally presided over the meeting and in particular dispensed a collection of quite valuable prizes; very often this lady was hostess for the day, as more often than not the shooting took place in the grounds of her country home. Long before this, when the medieval joust and tourney became an elaborate social occasion, each contestant would be favoured by the patronage of a lady to inspire him to greater feats of arms. This was in keeping with the chivalric ideals of the day when knights would face ordeals for honour and his lady alone. It appears that the lady for whom the highest-ranking knight fought became the Lady Paramount, but her actual duties, apart from being a decoration and an inspiration, are not altogether clear. Somewhere along the line the archery patroness took the earlier title of her medieval ancestor and nowadays we have

E

presiding at all our archery meetings a Lady Paramount. Today there is an echo of chivalry in the fact that officially the Lady Paramount has command of the archery meeting which she has consented to patronize and it is to her that an ultimate appeal is directed.

Usually an approach is made to a distinguished lady archer to act as Lady Paramount but there is no official objection to a lady taking this office who is not a practising archer. It will readily be seen, however, that it is desirable that she should have some knowledge of or interest in the sport. This is a traditional office and the absence of a radiant Lady Paramount congratulating prizewinners and encouraging those not so fortunate, adding extra charm to our colourful archery scene, would leave a void which would be hard to fill.

The choice of Judge—who, incidentally, is not allowed to participate in the shooting—will materially affect the success of any tournament. Once the first arrow is away he is in complete charge of shooting, and it is patent that he should have a precise and exact knowledge of the *Rules of Shooting*; he should be able to command respect and gently but firmly maintain order. He should be able to make spot decisions and be able to answer queries on the many contingencies which are not allowed for, such as bad weather or accidents (which fortunately are almost non-existent in this country); he is the final arbiter on the field and in all his is a very great responsibility. Fortunate indeed are the tournament organizers who can secure the services of such a paragon, and it is recommended that special arrangements should be made on his behalf such as transport to a ground which may well be strange to him, a careful briefing as to the policy of the particular meeting which he is to control and possibly relieving him of the worry of having to find his own lunch.

The appointment of a Field Captain at archery tournaments can often relieve the Judge of a number of tasks. Again this official should have a comprehensive knowledge of shooting rules and tournament procedure. He is likewise not permitted to take part in the actual shooting.

Recruiting helpers

Many and varied are the tasks which confront the tournament organizer, and it is practically an impossibility for one individual to do everything. It is therefore to his advantage to find voluntary helpers who will assist with some of the mundane tasks, leaving him free to concentrate on the more exacting work. Such essential aspects as measuring up and laying out the ground should be under his supervision, but the services of a couple of willing assistants can make the task much lighter. In this respect it is also helpful to have a second check on measurements so that accuracy can be guaranteed.

If the ground chosen is normally used by a local club there is usually little difficulty in securing help; on the other hand if the ground is not normally used for archery purposes a friendly groundsman may consent to give up an hour or so of his time. In such a case a gratuity would be appropriate.

The recruitment of helpers can often result in disappointment as some folk, with the best of intentions, having pledged themselves to assist, find that at the last minute there is a very good reason why they cannot fulfil their promise. This is the worst that can happen but invariably there always seems to be someone ready to step in and fill the breach.

The accurate compilation of results calls for helpers of a special kind. A small but efficient team of three or four will usually be sufficient to produce a set of results in a reasonable time for a normal archery tournament. Some further notes of this specialized aspect are mentioned below when 'field arrangements' are discussed.

Supply of equipment

More often than not targets and stands have to be hired or borrowed from clubs in the district and this is a matter which should have early attention. The estimated number of targets and stands required should be ascertained and their availability assured. Careful arrangements should be made for their transport, and if possible they should be inspected beforehand to ensure that they are in good condition and suitable for tournament use. Hire charges should be agreed and the whole matter confirmed just prior to the day they are required.

Catering and extra features

When an archer enters for a tournament he likes to know of any arrangements made for catering and special consideration should be given to this problem. Quite often personal picnic meals are preferred but regular supplies of refreshments are welcomed and the organizers would do well to investigate the possibilities of such facilities. Sometimes it is possible to offer luncheons and in this case prepayment is usually requested at the time of entry. Coffee and tea served on the shooting line is popular and an inclusive charge is often made to cover this. A licensed bar in a marquee or pavilion can be a great asset to a large meeting, and the general comfort and convenience of the competitors must be studied so that they are not without anything they are likely to need.

Novel features often make a special occasion of an otherwise normal function and organizing bodies will no doubt have ideas of their own in this respect. Care must be taken, of course, not to introduce anything which will affect the smooth running of the meeting or offend the good taste of the competitors. Popular at many meetings is a colourful display of club banners on elaborate poles erected behind the shooting line—these are known as 'Gonfalons'—and they provide a focal point of interest and conversation. For special meetings, such as anniversary meetings, commemorative badges have been issued, which although primarily of souvenir interest have a publicity value for that particular meeting. Distinguished personalities have been invited to open tournaments by shooting the first arrow, and despite hasty and concentrated coaching beforehand have gained the sympathy of all those present by their good-humoured awkwardness. Short religious services have been conducted immediately before the commencement of a meeting and social activities such as film shows, suppers, and dances have been arranged to take place in the evening after shooting. All these innovations and many more will no doubt be introduced by enterprising and ingenious organizers, serving to make present-day archery meetings more attractive.

2. Publicity

The notes that follow cover the most important aspect of any function—the means by which it is advertised, without which there would be no meeting. Once a tournament has been planned its publicity has to be decided and it is obvious that this will vary considerably according to the scale and character of the meeting.

A club shoot need only have personal publicity in the form of a notice to members informing them of the relevant details. Other methods of advising the archery public of a future tournament will be applied according to the needs of the organizers. Such mediums include columns in newsletters and bulletins published by the G.N.A.S. and a 'Dates to Remember' feature in the *British Archer* both of which have a national coverage, the former being issued free to clubs affiliated to the G.N.A.S. and the latter supplied on order. Certain regional bodies and county associations publish newsletters which invariably include notices of forthcoming events and these are excellent for publicising a meeting. There are advantages to be gained in a direct approach to archers through their club secretaries.

As much notice as possible is desirable so that individuals can plan their season's activities well in advance. Some tournaments include an announcement at the prizegiving of the date of the following year's meeting, and it is not unusual to see permanent dates booked as a feature of a particular tournament. The first announcement need only be quite brief and should include the name of the meeting, whether the prizes are to be awarded on an 'open' basis or restricted to local competitors, the date it is to be held and the tournament secretary's name and address. Extra information can be added if required, but greater detail is normally supplied by issuing a prospectus and entry form on application.

The entry form and prospectus

The preparation of the prospectus and entry form must be carefully attended to and the instructions and information given therein should be concise and without ambiguity. Naturally the details shown will vary according to the specific requirements of the individual meeting but these should include full particulars of the place, date and time, the rounds and awards, entry fees, the officials and the organizing body together with any special conditions applicable, those eligible to enter, and finally administrative notes including travel directions, parking facilities, catering and other relevant particulars. It is usual for the prospectus to be separate from the entry form so that it can be retained by the archer.

The entry form should be as simple and straightforward as possible and the competitor who will be responsible for completing this will appreciate the minimum 'form filling' in addition to enough space to complete the details required. Time taken in the preparation of a well-planned entry form will show practical dividends, for apart from the good impression this creates such forms can be used for administrative and record purposes.

Editors of local newspapers will welcome an advance notice of a meeting and will usually arrange for a reporter and possibly a photographer to attend some time during the day. This is just one more matter for the tournament organizer to attend to, and he should make available as much information as required—it is sometimes quite convenient to have some notes already typed to be used as a 'handout'—and he should provide as many facilities as possible so that an accurate and full account of the meeting can be reported. Be ready to provide full results—and don't be too indignant if your tournament does not make the front page.

The taking of photographs should be controlled so as not to distract or interfere with the competitors in any way. For the obvious reasons of safety under G.N.A.S. rules no archer is allowed to pose with loaded bow except on the shooting line and aiming at the target, and photographs taken from in front of the shooting line should be forbidden. By all means encourage official photographers who will single out pretty girls, local personalities or eccentric garb for their subjects.

Target lists

To compile a target list to suit everybody is almost an impossibility but a sincere effort must be made to accommodate competitors according to their particular desires as far as possible. It is customary to include a space to be completed on the entry form which indicates whether the archer is left-handed or right-handed (this applies to the way a bow is held, a right-handed archer holds the bow in his *left* hand and vice versa) and often an invitation is extended to competitors to suggest their target companions. These two facts plus quite a lot of other details can pave the way to the successful arrangement of a target list. It is not good enough to lump all the archers shooting one particular round together without consideration of the fact that they have to spend the whole day in the company of four or five other archers on their particular target. What then are the points that should be considered when planning a target list? Two have already been mentioned; if the archer is left-handed it is only fair, and for practical reasons much more convenient, to put him with the other left-handers on the left of the shooting line. This means that all those shooting with their bows in their right hands will face the same way, the remainder will therefore be facing the opposite direction. There should be no objection to the grouping together of personal friends who request such an arrangement, unless of course it means that a particular target becomes overloaded. Some archers have a preference for shooting in the middle of the shooting line or toward one end or the other, again there should be no reason why this caprice cannot be attended to. Careful selection of target captains, the third archer to shoot on each target, can be an advantage, for if it is known that a certain individual habitually makes errors or gets worried or harassed by this duty it is far better to allocate the position to another archer. It is far more enjoyable to shoot with companions of one's own standard, and by discrimination the correct balance can be obtained, giving the Master Bowman an opportunity of matching his skill against other Master Bowmen and allowing the less qualified archer to shoot with other archers of his standard. In this connexion it is sound practice to allocate pairs of archers of comparable performance to shoot together. The target list should include any special instructions concerning shooting, the place, date and time of the meeting and the names of the officials. Distribution can be made to individual entrants a week or ten days before the shoot and copies must be reserved for the Lady Paramount, the Judges, the Field Captain and for official use.

3. Field arrangements

The ideal layout of a ground for a tournament is shown in Fig. 42, but it is by no means a hard and fast pattern and variations will be made to suit local conditions and individual preferences.

Care should be taken to see the ground is 'squared' before any layout is begun, and it is advisable to start by establishing a base line from which all measurements can be taken. The most convenient base on which to work is the shooting line and once this has been pegged out a further line can be added at an angle of ninety degrees. The requisite shooting distances can be measured along this line and pegged out; a line on which the targets will be set can then be marked. The fourth side of the rectangle then acts as a double check on the geometry so far. Once confirmation is given of the accuracy of the lines that have been laid the individual target positions can be marked with corresponding marks on the shooting line. Finally the lesser distances are marked and target stands erected.

The targets can be arranged in different ways and this must be planned beforehand; the simplest is to have an evenly spaced line with the regulation distance between target centres. An alternative method which has often been recommended is to have groups of three targets separated by wider gaps, yet another variant is to have ladies' and gentlemen's targets arranged alternately. Setting up the target stands calls for a regimental

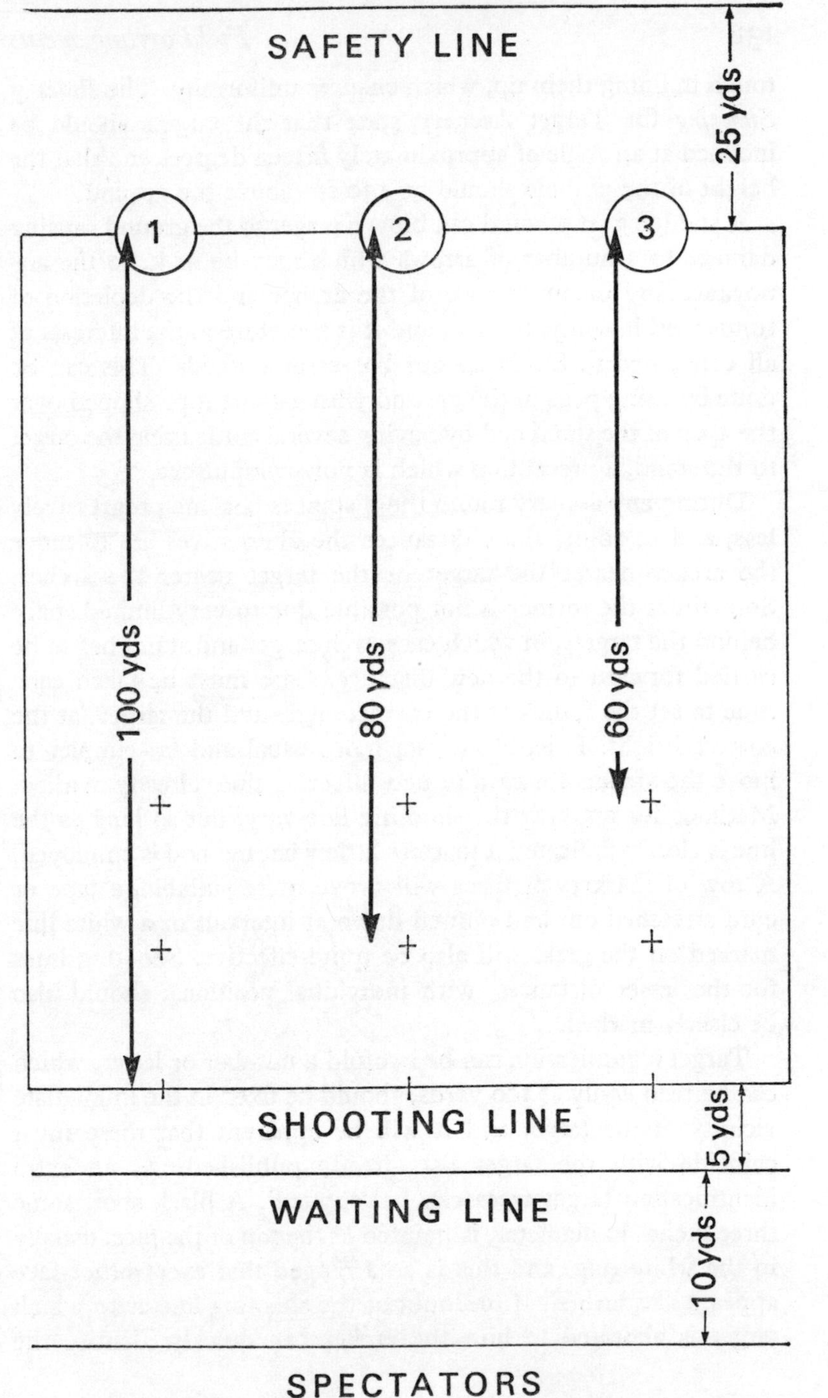

Fig. 42 Typical layout of an archery field

touch in lining them up, which ensures uniformity. The *Rules of Shooting* for Target Archery state that the targets should be inclined at an angle of approximately fifteen degrees and that the height of the pinhole should be 130 cm above the ground.

A sudden gust of wind can blow a target to the ground causing damage to a number of arrows which may be in it, to the annoyance and inconvenience of the archer and the depletion of funds paid in compensation, and it is therefore in the interests of all concerned to firmly anchor bosses and stands. This can be done by using pegs in the ground with a short rope slipped over the apex of the stand and by having several cords tying the target to the stand, a precaution which is now compulsory.

During any archery round the distances become progressively less, and to adjust these distances the alternatives are to move the archer nearer the target or the target nearer the archer. Sometimes the former is not possible due to very limited space behind the targets, in which case each target and stand has to be carried forward to the new distance. Care must be taken each time to set the stands at the correct angle and the targets at the correct height. It is, of course, more usual and far simpler to move the archers forward to new shooting lines already marked. Methods for marking the shooting line vary, but so long as the line is clearly indicated it matters little what method is employed. A row of markers or discs will prove quite suitable, a tape or cord stretched out and pinned down at intervals or a white line marked on the grass will also be quite effective. Shooting lines for the lesser distances, with individual positions, should also be clearly marked.

Target identification can be twofold a number or letter, which can be read easily at 100 yards, should be fixed in the immediate vicinity of the target and it will be apparent that these must coincide with the target list already published. As an extra identification target faces can be 'spotted'. A black spot, some three inches in diameter, is painted at the top of the face, usually in the white ring, and this is so arranged that every other face appears so adorned. If in doubt at the shooting line as to which target is allocated to him the archer can quickly identify the correct one by observing both these markings. The target face should ideally present a virgin surface at the start of each tournament but costs will often prevent this. As an alternative ensure that the faces used are the best that can be supplied and above all are uniform in appearance. A proportion of the outlay on new target faces can sometimes be recovered by selling off used faces at the end of the day at bargain prices, but the supply of this commodity in recent years has outstripped the demand and one cannot rely on this source of revenue.

A British champion was once heard to say that the only problem organizers of archery tournaments did not face was the question of lavatory facilities. This, of course, is not true but let it be said that it is a point which needs to be high on the list of priorities. Suitably distinct notices and directional signs should be used including those indicating the existence of barriers to spectators as well as competitors, which will be greatly appreciated, and incidentally ease the officials of the exasperating task of giving directions throughout the day.

Timing

Throughout the meeting, progress should be checked against the previously estimated timing, which may be upset by weather conditions, so as to plan well ahead for refreshment breaks, prizegiving times and other administration. To commence the shoot late is to get off to a bad start and the time lost can rarely be made up. Each minute in arrears increases the impatience and frustration of the competitors. This also applies to the recommencement of shooting after lunch (which incidentally should be arranged between distances), and the time allowed for breaks must be clearly announced and strictly adhered to. Prizegiving can be preceded by an awkward gap in the proceedings, particularly if the tired and homesick archers are left to their own devices for an unspecified period of time. Far better to announce that the results will be ready by such a time and arrange that tea can be obtained in the interval, and a display of prizes and awards at this stage can also be popular. If the results are ready before the time stated it is unfair to spring a surprise by announcing them early. Further mention of the actual presentation arrangements is given below when post-tournament procedures are discussed.

Scoring

The basic aim of a scores team is to receive complete individual score sheets, and to extract a correct list of results according to a pre-arranged pattern. How is this to be worked simply and smoothly so that this task is completed in the minimum time without error and without the necessity of repeated checking? One essential is to have a Chief Scorer, to give a name to the person in charge, to co-ordinate the work and direct each stage of the analysis with due regard to the requirements of the meeting.

4. Post-tournament procedure

The prizegiving

Some note has already been made of the importance of adhering to a previously announced timetable. By the appointed hour for the presentation of awards the general audience should be assembled, seated if possible, and on a platform or dais the Lady Paramount, Tournament Organizer and Chairman in their places behind the prize table. A simple procedure which will admirably suit the occasion is as follows: the Chairman opens the proceedings with a short address, which includes a vote of thanks to all those involved in organizing and running the tournament, he then introduces the Lady Paramount and concludes by asking her to present the prizes. Little need be said about the making of speeches but the Lady Paramount will appreciate a lead up to the 'few remarks' now expected of her.

It is quite surprising how minor details can escape the notice of organizers: one example being the way in which announcements are made for individual awards. The facts to be announced include the award, the name of the prizewinner and the club to which he belongs, and the score. Care should be taken to reserve the name until last, otherwise essential details, such as the score, will be drowned in applause. The announcement should therefore be something like this: 'The winner of the Blanksville Cup for the highest score in the York round, with 144 hits, a score of 1000 and 50 golds, from the Blankers Archery Club, is Mr. A. Blank.' The usual procedure of handing over the correct award then takes place. Often with a number of quite similar medals in exactly similar boxes it is a good plan to number the box to correspond with a numbered list of awards. Mistakes can occur and if the organizer realizes that an error in presentaton has been made, or if during prizegiving a query arises, it is far better to continue as though nothing had happened, sorting out the problem afterwards. If valuable trophies are involved it may be thought desirable to obtain a signature from the prizewinner in a trophy book, and again this can be dealt with after the prize-giving. Finally a delightful custom which should be preserved, a small presentation should be made to the Lady Paramount of a sheaf of flowers or something suitable for the occasion, preferably by the Lady Champion of the day or alternatively by the youngest archer present or a suitably self-confident tot.

Little can be said about clearing the field that is not obvious, but it must not be forgotten that the activity behind the scenes will be at its highest pitch just at the time when help is needed to clear all targets, stands, markers, rubbish and inevitable lost property. Let us hope that the organizer had foreseen this and was able to recruit sufficient labour to help out at this stage. It is only courtesy to leave the ground as it was found, and if by accident any damage occurred during the day, this should now be reported.

Publishing results

The penultimate task of the tournament organizer is to prepare and distribute the results to all concerned, which not only includes all competitors but also the willing helpers and officials who contributed to the success of the tournament. The results should also be sent to editors of newspapers, archery journals and newsletters as necessary. The standard type of score sheet includes the main awards as announced at the prizegiving plus a complete list of all competitors, showing their positions according to 'made' scores. Those who entered and for some reason could not attend or did not complete the day's shooting should also be shown as having entered. Some factual notes are often added including weather conditions, any exceptional events that may have happened during the day and the date of the next meeting, if this is known. It is recommended that the greatest care should be taken in compiling the results sheet as this then becomes the official record of the meeting. It is a mistake to boast efficiency in the preparation and distribution of a results sheet in record time if it is inaccurate or incomplete. Far better to assume that the competitor is prepared to wait patiently for a day or so longer in the anticipation of the concise and correct record.

What else remains? Tying up loose ends such as official 'thank you' letters, returning borrowed equipment and 'dealing with the account'. The latter will entail more or less work according to the scale of the meeting, but in all cases a separate account should be prepared for each tournament. Methods will vary, but whatever the system the organizer's task cannot be considered complete until final figures are produced. He can then congratulate himself on the success of the meeting, take a deep breath and start preparation for the next.

These notes, sketchy in places and elementary in others, are intended to indicate basic procedure for a meeting of any size. Further elaboration or modification of the practical, administrative, or social aspects of your particular tournament can only be made by experience and the conjunction of theory and practice.

9 · Archery International

The steady growth of archery as an international sporting pursuit since the Second World War has been due to several factors. The most significant cause has been the standardization of shooting arrangements and the regularization of rules for competition. Contributory factors include the availability of a greater variety of improved equipment, easier and quicker communication and travel, and a desire for relaxation from the hurly-burly of the modern world, made possible by more leisure time. The wider participation in the sport has been encouraged by the lowering of class barriers, a social phenomenon common to other sports and pursuits. Archery was formerly considered to be reserved for the upper middle classes with time and money to spare, and the notion that archery was rather 'precious', a hangover from the Victorian era, has now been completely dispelled, and men and women from every class and occupation enjoy the pleasures of shooting in a bow more than ever before. Much could also be said about the benefits of people of different nationalities, with dissimilar cultures and conflicting ideologies, meeting together for a common purpose, utilizing skills which can be understood universally, and sharing the same ideals of competition. In this there can be recognized the fundamental principles of the Olympic Games, which are eminently desirable for the promotion of a greater understanding amongst nations.

However, none of this would have been possible without the untiring efforts of the International Archery Federation (Fédération Internationale de Tir à l'Arc) or F.I.T.A. as it is generally known, who have unified the many different ways in which modern competitive archery has been pursued, and this body has given to the sport a new and popular image. The beginnings of international archery, as we know it today, can be confidently assigned to 1931, when Poland took the initiative and held an International Tournament at Lwòw. It was during that year that F.I.T.A. was instituted to act as a central authority

Fig. 43 The F.I.TA. badge

for archery with four original members, Belgium, France, Poland, and Sweden. Great Britain joined the Federation the following year, and since then membership has gradually grown until today there are nearly sixty national amateur associations who are affiliated to that parent body. The first object of F.I.T.A. is to 'promote and encourage archery throughout the world', and this is put into practice through the organization of World Championships and other continental or regional championships in any branch of archery and by framing and interpreting rules of shooting.

The ultimate achievement for a competitive archer is to reach world championship standard, and the path to such heights is a steady climb through club, county, regional, and national competition. The history of world championships can be related to the early participation in the Olympic Games by relatively small groups of archers. Usually, as the Games moved from country to country and continent to continent, it was the archers who lived in the host countries who formed the majority of the competitors. For example the IVth Olympiad of 1908, held in London, saw forty British, eleven French, and one lone competitor from America. It is not surprising that this situation persisted, as the inclusion of archery as an event at successive Games was included at the request of the national archery association of the countries where the Games were held. International rules did not exist, so the national rules of the host country were used. In the early 1900s a series of ambitious International Archery Meetings were run at Le Touquet, and attempts were made to establish an 'international' round which could be shot at all such meetings. Although there are no records of this round being shot at other than these meetings, which were curtailed by the First World War, the idea of an international round which could be used for competition throughout the world had been established.

The need to regularize rules and to standardize shooting arrangements was vital if any comparisons were to be made between the performance of archers of different nationalities. It was by following this precept that, after various changes and amendments, the current F.I.T.A. Rounds were devised, and the regulations for internal archery were laid down. The arrangements for shooting so devised have not superseded 'national' rules, particularly in so far as specific rounds are concerned, but in the last few years more interest has been taken by rank and file members of clubs throughout Britain and elsewhere in shooting F.I.T.A. Rounds. The reason for this is clear, many of the meetings held under the auspices of most member associations are organized so that F.I.T.A. rules apply. This has several implications. For example postal matches can be conducted between clubs from different countries, in which case F.I.T.A. Rounds are shot and scores exchanged by post. There is also the encouragement for individuals to enter major competitions with the extra distinction of gaining F.I.T.A. Star badges for special prowess and becoming eligible for selection for championship and Olympic teams.

The World Target Championships are held every second year and the titles of Champion of the World and Lady Champion of the World are awarded to those archers who succeed in making the top scores of two F.I.T.A. Rounds, which were introduced as standard championship rounds in 1957. For ladies the distances are 70, 60, 50 and 30 metres, and for gentlemen they are 90, 70, 50 and 30 metres, and thirty-six arrows are shot at each distance on 80-cm targets for the shorter distances and 122-cm targets for the longer. In each case the targets are divided into ten concentric scoring zones with values of 1 to 10.

Up to 1967 the locations for the championships were exclusively European and the winners were drawn predominantly from those countries in which the meetings were held, although by that time membership of F.I.T.A. included archery associations from North and South America, Asia and Australasia. The following table shows the relationship between the nationality of the winners of World Championships and the country in which they were held.

World Championships

	Host country	*Nationality of champions*	
		Ladies	*Gentlemen*
1931	Poland	Poland	Poland
1932	Poland	Poland	Belgium
1933	Great Britain	Poland	USA
1934	Sweden	Poland	Sweden
1935	Belgium	Sweden	Belgium
1936	Czechoslovakia	Poland	Sweden
1937	France	Great Britain	Belgium
1938	Great Britain	Great Britain	Czechoslovakia
1939	Sweden	Poland	France
1946	Sweden	Great Britain	Denmark
1947	Czechoslovakia	Poland	Sweden
1948	Great Britain	Great Britain	Sweden
1949	France	Great Britain	Sweden
1950	Denmark	USA	Sweden
1952	Belgium	USA	Sweden
1953	Norway	USA	Sweden
1955	Finland	Poland	Sweden
1957	Czechoslovakia	USA	USA
1958	Belgium	Sweden	Sweden
1959	Sweden	USA	USA
1961	Norway	USA	USA
1963	Finland	USA	USA

	Host country	*Nationality of champions*	
		Ladies	*Gentlemen*
1965	Sweden	Finland	Finland
1967	Netherlands	Poland	USA
1969	USA	Canada	USA
1971	Great Britain	USSR	USA
1973	France	USA	USSR
1975	Switzerland	USSR	USA
1977	Australia	USA	USA

From this table it can be seen that as the shooting rules became more firmly established the winners were drawn from a wider membership, as opposed to the earlier situation when the winner often shot, so to speak, on his or her home ground. Many other interesting conclusions can be drawn from these and other records, although to make a thorough analysis many other factors would have to be considered, such as age groups, technical and stylistic considerations, the facilities and encouragement for training experienced by archers from different countries, and even climate and national temperament. This would not be entirely an academic exercise because such information could form useful guidelines for the general training and coaching of all archers.

Notable champions who held world titles for a number of years were Mrs. J. Spychyowa-Kurkowska from Poland, who secured the championship seven times, and Hans Deutgen of Sweden, who was World Champion four times. Mrs. P. Wharton-Burr of Great Britain and Miss J. Lee of America, each secured the champion's crown twice. The first World Championship meeting in 1931 is the only occasion in the history of the event when both winners represented the host country, Poland, and it was not until 1957 that both winners again came from the same country, in this case America, the meeting that year being held in Czechoslovakia. Another memorable occasion was in 1971 when Miss E. Gapchenko, of the Soviet Union, stood with John Williams from America as World Champions—a notable exercise in entente cordiale. In 1973 these rôles were reversed when Linda Myers of America and Viktor Sidoruk of the Soviet

Union won the coveted honours. This pattern was again reversed in 1975 when Miss Zebiniso Rustamova of the Soviet Union and Darrell Pace of America became World Champions. In these few years the highest achievements on the archery field were shared by representatives of the two great world powers, and in terms of human endeavour this was no less significant amongst archers of the world than the much publicized link-up in space in 1975 by Russian and American cosmonauts was to international scientists.

In addition to World Championships F.I.T.A. organize several other important events including continental/regional Target Championships and World Field Championships, held in the years when there is no World Target Championship, and an annual F.I.T.A. Mail Match. The Federation has powers delegated to it for the technical control of archery at the Olympic Games and it is represented on the International Olympic Committee. It is a short step from World Championships to the Olympics, but a step which has been taken in slow motion. The events which consisted of some forms of archery for the Games of 1900, 1904 and 1920 were not properly representative of international competitive archery. No universally accepted standard rules applied and the shooting that took place was more or less a concession to the host countries who employed their own particular national shooting formulas. For example metric distances were used for target shooting in Paris in 1900, and again in Antwerp in 1920, with additional popinjay and crossbow competitions. The meeting of 1904 in St. Louis, where the winners were entirely American, included a series of rounds normally used in that country. The IVth Olympiad held in London in 1908 compromised to a certain extent by including both imperial and metric distances for competition, and this meeting can be considered as a positive move towards the establishment of archery as an Olympic event. It was not until sixty-four years later, in 1972, at Munich, when archery was finally included in the XXth Olympiad with a strong international following and with firmly established standardized rules of shooting. Archers from twenty-eight countries, who had reached the required proficiency, thus celebrated the ultimate recognition of archery as a world-wide amateur sport.

Selection of British teams for international competition is based on proficiency, and under the system laid down by the Grand National Archery Society, each archery club affiliated to that body maintains a complete record of each member's scores, with a centralizing arrangement for team selection for county, regional, national and international tournaments. Other national organizations operate similar systems. Each year the G.N.A.S. Selection Committee nominate competitors for an International Trial, to which archers from other F.I.T.A. member associations are invited, and it is normally only competitors at this meeting who qualify for selection as members of British teams for World and European championships.

To become proficient in any sport it is necessary to have time to practise and to train; to be able to enter major competitive events it is necessary to be able to afford the cost of travel and accommodation. Both these matters are considered essential by some governments, who regard success in sport as being a national achievement, and accordingly they arrange to assist competitors in these and other problems. Other governments, possibly influenced by the traditions of privately sponsored sporting activities, are slower to respond to modern demands of this nature.

The eligibility code of the International Olympic Committee spells out the danger of creating pseudo-amateurs by subsidizing individuals because of their athletic ability, by governments, educational institutions or business concerns. It also points out that inducements of various kinds offered solely to create national aggrandizement, advertising promotions and prestige, conflict with the principles of amateurism, and therefore do not accord with the spirit and aims of the Olympic movement. This has certain implications in so far as archery is concerned, as in recent years various traditional sweepstakes at archery meetings have been dropped to avoid contravention of Olympic regulations, and thus the possibility of individuals becoming ineligible for Olympic competition has been avoided. Wagers, lotteries and sweepstakes were once accepted as part of the customary proceedings at most archery meetings. The traditional, 'gold sweep', which until recently was an invariable feature of major tournaments, invited competitors to pay an equal share at the commencement of shooting and, according to the number of golds scored that day, they were paid out proportionately. Another custom was the payment of a pre-decimal shilling by all competitors shooting the same round to the archer who scored six consecutive golds—a perfect end. Nowadays the official recognition of this achievement is the award of a Six Gold Badge, which has to be gained at distances of at least 60 yards for ladies and 80 yards for gentlemen, or at the 70- and 60-metre and 90- and 70-metre distances respectively.

The changed status of archery in a comparatively short time, as has been shown by the above notes, is important to the newcomer. Anyone taking up the bow has the satisfaction of knowing that the support of a highly organized and efficient international federation reaches even the smallest club and, whereas it has taken a generation or so for archery to become firmly established internationally, it is not uncommon for archers themselves to reach championship standard in a surprisingly short time. Elsewhere in this book junior archers and disabled archers have been discussed, and the inexperience of youth and the handicap of disability are no disqualifications for international championship participation. For example at the 1973 World Championships at Grenoble the competitors included thirteen-year-old Jodi Crowl, who finished in tenth place, and several other competitors in their late teens such as the previous nineteen-year-old World Champion John Williams, now turned professional. Also at this meeting was Willie Kokott, shooting from a wheel-chair. The most exacting trials of an archer's skill are not restricted to those from a certain age group, or for that matter to powerful athletic types, and this is probably one of the most appealing aspects of the sport.

It must be said that in many ways an early introduction to archery is a great advantage, as it is in many sports, and the National Archery Association of America, conscious of this fact and interested in building a team for future Olympics, has instituted the Junior Olympic Archery Development Program. A special development course has been devised and is recommended for club, school and camp competition, and this is already proving extremely successful. Whereas youth requires guidance, the disciplines necessary for a beginner to become a champion can be self-imposed by adults, and a high degree of proficiency is frequently achieved in a surprisingly short time. Two to three seasons is not an unusual period for an archer to reach a relatively high standard.

Professional archery is a subject somewhat outside the scope of this book, but the Professional Archers Association of America deserves a brief mention for the important part it plays in publicizing the sport through commercial promotion and widely advertised competition. Many members of this association run their own businesses, which are directly connected with archery, and others are managers of pro.-shops in indoor archery lanes. A few are referees at the large indoor tournaments, and about half act as instructors at archery lanes in their own establishments and in clubs and camps. They therefore provide an extremely valuable service to archery by their promotional and training activities. There are professional archers in other countries who largely perform the same functions. In accordance with the ruling embodied in the eligibility code of the Olympic Committee, professional archers are excluded from competing at the Games.

The rules of shooting which are relevant to international competition are comprehensive, and include details for Target Archery, Field Archery and Clout Shooting. These, together with other information applicable to international competition, are included in F.I.T.A. *Constitution and Rules* which are regularly brought up-to-date and are readily available through club and regional secretaries.

'Many arrows loosed several ways'

When looking at a book for the first time some people thumb the last few pages to see how it ends, whereas others, who are not so inquisitive, patiently read each chapter and arrive later but wiser.

Different people approach archery in different ways. Matters which perplex some are straightforward for others, many enjoy experimentation but a great number prefer to follow well-defined patterns and, much as some find their pleasures in diverse forms of shooting, a proportion practise only one type of archery. Variations in technique are endless and the complexities of equipment can be bewildering but, master or novice, the ultimate aim of every archer is exactly the same—the everlasting search for some degree of achievement. Whether this be complete mastery or just slight betterment, it becomes an entirely personal matter.

Archers have an insatiable thirst for knowledge of their pursuit and if this book has sketched in the outlines of this fascinating subject for beginners and filled in some of the colours on this enormous canvas for the expert then its purpose has been fulfilled. The sentiments of an unknown sixteenth-century author are echoed in conclusion: 'And as I know that many take a pleasure in archery, I have resolved to write some things down. Not that I am fully aware that there are many who know more about it than I do, but solely because I wish that every one should become a good archer, begging that if there are faults they may be corrected, and that whatever may be found useful, may be taken in good part.'

Appendix A

Target Rounds

Name of Round	*Number of Arrows* 100 yd.	80 yd.	60 yd.	50 yd.	40 yd.	30 yd.	20 yd.
York	72	48	24				
St. George	36	36	36				
New Western	48	48					
New National	48	24					
Hereford (Bristol I)		72	48	24			
Long Western		48	48				
Long National		48	24				
Albion		36	36	36			
Windsor			36	36	36		
American			30	30	30		
Western			48	48			
National			48	24			
Junior Rounds							
Bristol I		72	48	24			
Bristol II			72	48	24		
Bristol III				72	48	24	
Bristol IV					72	48	24
Short Windsor				36	36	36	
St. Nicholas					48	36	

Metric Rounds	90 m	70 m	60 m	50 m	40 m	30 m	20 m	10 m
FITA (Gentlemen)	36	36		36		36		
FITA (Ladies) (Metric I)		36	36	36		36		
Long Metric (Gentlemen)	36	36						

Name of Round	*Number of Arrows*							
	90 m	*70 m*	*60 m*	*50 m*	*40 m*	*30 m*	*20 m*	*10 m*
Long Metric (Ladies)		36	36					
Short Metric				36		36		
Junior Rounds								
Metric I		36	36	36		36		
Metric II			36	36	36	36		
Metric III				36	36	36	36	
Metric IV					36	36	36	36

Indoor Rounds	*20 yd.*	*30 m*	*25 m*	*18 m*
Portsmouth (60 cm target face)	60			
Worcester (40 cm target face)	60			
Stafford (80 cm target face)		72		
FITA Round I (40 cm target face)				30
FITA Round II (60 cm target face)			30	

Notes

(a) In every round the longer, or longest distance, is shot first, and the shorter, or shortest distance, last.

(b) When FITA and Metric rounds are shot, FITA Rules apply.

(c) A FITA round may be shot in one day or over two consecutive days.

(d) All other rounds to be shot in one day. (Except in the case of a championship of more than one day's duration.)

Appendix B

USEFUL ADDRESSES

Grand National Archery Society
National Agricultural Centre, Stoneleigh, Kenilworth, CU8 2LG.

Association for Archery in Schools
Secretary: Mr. C. Fletcher-Campbell, Radley College, Abingdon, OX 14.

British Longbow Society
Secretary: Mr. R. D. Barnsdale, Manor Farm House, Dockenfield, Farnham, Surrey.

British Crossbow Society
Secretary: Mr. S. Turner, Rose Cottage, Derby Road, Tupton, Chesterfield.

National Field Archery Society
Secretary: Mr. R. Bickerstaffe, 67 Seaburn Road, Toton, Beeston, Notts. NG9 6HN.

National Coaching Organizer
Mr. Ellis Shepherd, 4 Park Drive, Rhyl, Clwyd, LL18 4DB.

National Film Library
Mr. J. Adams, 132 Hampstead Hall Road, Hadsworth Wood, Birmingham, 20.

Society of Archer-Antiquaries
Editor: Mr. Edward McEwen, 10 Richmond Way, Wanstead, London, E.11.

British Archer (published bi-monthly)
Technical Indexes Ltd., East Hampstead Road, Bracknell, Berkshire, RG12 1NS.

Index

advertising, 133
affiliation, 109–11
aiming, 88–91
aiming off, 47, 91
amateur status, 149
Anchor Point, 75
Archer-Antiquaries, Society of, 37
Archer's Notes, An, 57
Archer's Paradox, The, 21–2
Archery Achievement Scheme, 33
archery clubs, 109
Archery Darts, 43–4
Archery Golf, 50–1
Archery, its Theory and Practice, 57
arrows:
  alloy, 18
  barrelled, 45
  checking length, 25
  fibre-glass, 23
  flight, 48
  length of, 24
  parts of, 23
  retrieving, 107
  weight, 24
  wooden, 18
arrow flight, 22
arrow-rest, 19, 22
Ascham, Roger, 37, 56–7, 61–3, 65, 71, 76, 75–80, 99
Asiatic composite bow, 14, 16
  cross-section of, 16
automated range, 43
awards and prizes, 127–9

Basic Method, 55
best golds, 127
bow:
  Asiatic composite, 14, 16
  back of, 14
  backing, 16
  belly of, 14
  composite, 16
  fibre-glass, 27
  flat, 15
  flight, 49
  limbs, interchangeable, 18
  parts of, 19
  'stacked', 14
  steel, 15
  take-apart, 18
bow handle, 17, 19
bow stringer, 61
bowstrings, 27, 28
bracer, 28
bracing, 59
bracing height, 59, 69
Bristol School of Rounds, 33
British Archer, 133
British Colour Council, 31
British Crossbow Society, 37
British Longbow Society, 37
butt shooting, 39

Carew, Richard, 98
challenge trophies, 127
Classification Scheme, 115–17
clicker, 93
Clout Shooting, 44–5
club rules, 120
Club Target Day, 116

coaching, 37–8
cock feather, 27
composite bow, 16
  cross-section of, 17
constitutions for club, 120–3
creeping, 79
cresting, 26
Crowl, Jodi, 150

demonstrations, 112
Deutgen, Hans, 147
disabled archers, 34–6
dominant eye, 86
draw weights, 27
drawing, 71
dress regulations, 103
Duke of Edinburgh's Award Scheme, 33

Edwards, C. B., 57
elevation of arrow, 90
'end' of arrows, 42
equipment, selection of, 22
etiquette, 101

'Fast', 104
faults, 94
fibre-glass, 27
Field Archery, 45–7
Field Captain, 102
field layout, 137
Finsbury Archers, 40
Finsbury Fields, 52
Fédération Internationale de Tir à l'Arc (F.I.T.A.), 110, 117, 127, 143–6, 148–9
F.I.T.A., *Constitution and Rules*, 151
F.I.T.A. Stars, 145
fitness, 100
flat bow, 15
fletchings, 25
flight bow, 49
Flight Shooting, 47–9
Follow Through, 84
foot markers, 65
Ford, H. A., 57
freezing, 84–91
full-draw, 75

Gapchenko, Miss E., 147
gonfalons, 132
Grand Master Bowman, 116
Grand National Archery Society, G.N.A.S., 109–11, 113, 116–17
G.N.A.S. *Rules of Shooting*, 43, 103–4, 120
Guttman, Dr., 35

Handicap Scheme, 115–17
Hickman, C. N., 14
holding, 76

Indoor Shooting 43
instinctive aiming, 91
instructors, 38
insurance, 110
internationalism, 143
International Trial, 149

Judge, 102, 130
Junior Championships, 33

Kilwinning Archers, Ancient Society of, 50
Klopsteg, P. E., 14
Kokot, Willie, 150

Lady Paramount, 129
Lee, Miss J., 147
Le Touquet meetings, 48, 145
Line of Direction, 89
Line of Flight, 89
Line of Sight, 89
Longbow, 14
  cross-section of, 14
loosing, 79

maintenance, 106
Master Bowman, 116
measuring card, 128
Mediterranean loose, 30
membership, 111
multiple fletching, 25
Myers, Linda, 147

National Archery Association of America, 150

National Association of Archery Coaches, 38
National Coaching Organization, 38
National Film Library, 37
National Indoor Championship Meeting, 43
nocking, 65–7
nocking point, 28
nocks, 14
novelty shooting, 52

Olympic Games, 143–4
over-bowed, 93
over-drawing, 95

Pace, Darrell, 148
Paraplegic Games, 35
parts of an arrow, 23
parts of a bow, 19
perfect end, 101
pinhole, 42
point-of-aim, 47
Popinjay Shooting, 49–50
postal matches, 145
Preparation Line, 70
Preparation Position, 70
Prince's Reckoning, the, 40
prizegiving, 140
Professional Archers' Association of America, 151
psychology of archery, 97–100
publicity, 111, 133

quiver, 30

Records Officer, 115
recurves, 20
rounds, 40, 42
Rovers, 51–3
Royal Company of Archers, 44
Rustamova, Zebiniso, 148

safety, 103–6
schools archery, 33
score sheet, 123
scoring values, 42
semi-centre shot bow, 19
serving, 28
shooting field, 104
shooting line, 106, 138
shooting tab, 29
Sidoruk, Viktor, 147
sight, use of, 91
sighters, 42
sighting device, 90
Six Gold Badge, 150
spine, 23
spiralled fletching, 25
Spychyowa-Kurkowska, Mrs. J. 147
stabilizers, 17
standing, 61–4
steel bow, 15
subscriptions, 118

take-apart bow, 18
Target Archery, 39–43
Target Captain, 102
target:
  colours, 40
  faces, 42
  lists, 135
tassel, 30
Tassel Register, 31
team selection, 149
thumb ring, 48
Timber Hitch, 27
torque, 17, 96
tournament procedure, 124
Toxophilus, 56
traditions, 119
trajectory, 89
two-way shooting, 41

under-drawing, 96
unwritten rules, 101

vision, 86–8
visual defects, 87–8

Wharton-Burr, Mrs. P., 147
Williams, John, 147
Woodmen of Arden, 44
World Champions, 146
World Field Championships, 148
World Target Championships, 144